D1785754

DIRTY TALK:
Conversations with Porn Stars

DIRTY TALK:
Conversations with Porn Stars

by Andrew J. Rausch and Chris Watson

BearManor Media

2012

Dirty Talk: Conversations with Porn Stars

© 2011 Andrew J. Rausch and Chris Watson

All rights reserved.

For information, address:

BearManor Media
P. O. Box 71426
Albany, GA 31708

bearmanormedia.com

Typesetting and layout by John Teehan
Cover designed by R. D. Riley

Published in the USA by BearManor Media

ISBN—1-59393-284-7
978-1-59393-284-8

TABLE OF CONTENTS

INTRODUCTION
by Ted Newsom

YOU'RE ABOUT TO READ a skewed version of the porn film industry.

That can't be helped. Every version of anything is skewed by the observer's point of view. The observer alters reality by the very act of observation; Schrödinger's Cat meowed that to me once. In this case, the observers are two guys named Rausch and Watson, and to skew reality one more level, the tales are told by ten different people who work in the adult film industry. All but one (the understandably bitter Kyle Stone) paint a matter-of-fact picture of their experiences in the sex biz.

Can that be true? Can performing sex for a living in front of a camera be as "normal" as they describe so flatly, so blithely? Sure it can. It's as "true" as the anti-porn screeds in print and video documentaries. Try getting two people to describe a traffic accident exactly the same way.

Is porn a bad thing? Stupid question. It's a thing. One set of cheerleaders will always rail that it debases a sacred act, screws up expectations of what real sex is like, degrades women (and the occasional innocent twink), makes millions for mobsters (Russian, Sicilian, Jewish and otherwise), and generally causes bad breath in dogs. The other team will respond that it is the public perception of sex which stinks, not the dog's breath; that prior to the glorious Christian conquest, sex was an accepted part of every society, from ancient Mesopotamia to Greece and Rome, from the Asian nations of yore to the woods of Europe.

"Is sex dirty?" asked Woody Allen rhetorically. He answered, "Yes, if it's done correctly."

I remember reading a friend's copy of the wildly-illustrated Report of the Commission on Obscenity and Pornography, ordered up under Lyndon Johnson in 1969 and received by Nixon in 1970. Bluenoses desper-

1

ately wanted a handbook to prove the evils of smut; what they received was a scholarly dissertation which stated the opposite, pointing out that incidences of sex crimes *dropped* dramatically in Denmark after porn and prostitution were legalized. Other annoying conclusions:

There was "no evidence to date that exposure to explicit sexual materials plays a significant role in the causation of delinquent or criminal behavior among youths or adults."

> "… [the] majority of American adults believe that adults should be allowed to read or see any sexual materials they wish."

> A complete lack of scientific or documentary "evidence that exposure to explicit sexual materials adversely affects character or moral attitudes regarding sex and sexual conduct."

> And most infuriatingly to the government, that "Federal, State, and Local legislation prohibiting the sale, exhibition, or distribution of sexual materials to consenting adults should be repealed."

Boy, was everybody pissed off, especially Charles Keating, a Nixon-appointed latecomer to the group and one of the few hard-core conservatives on the panel. That's the same hypocritical thief who masterminded the Lincoln Savings & Loan scandal, collapsing not only his own corrupt company to the tune of three billion dollars but taking 23,000 customers' chances of retirement with it. Keating did a measly four and a half year prison term for 73 counts of racketeering and fraud. I like to imagine the old bastard spending his spell in the iron motel getting tag-team ass-raped by two swarthy thugs named Bubba and Chuwey. It's the romantic in me.

Keating was serious about his porn crusade—suspiciously so. He was behind getting the innocuous comedy *O! Calcutta* banned, pressuring convenience stores to remove *Playboy* and assorted other stroke books, even trying to get the goofy movie *Vixen* labeled pornographic, calling director Russ Meyer "the most dangerous man in America." Oy. So serious was Keating in his clean-up mission that he kept a library of gross, outlandish porn in his office, showing it to anyone who questioned his motives.

Keating's handy porn stash and alleged dismay reminds me of the reaction of my boss in the U.S. Army optical clinic (in the quaint year of 1973, when pubic hair was a rarity in magazines). He saw a two page *Playboy* spread of Edy Williams (coincidentally shot by her husband, Russ Meyer), triangularly wanton and eye-poppingly spread-eagled in a swimming pool, her dark thatch on full display. "Disgraceful," said my 40-ish boss, an officer and an optometrist. I closed the magazine, and he opened it again for a closer look. "Has she no shame?" he asked, eyeing it carefully. No, sir, probably not.

And that reminds me of the joke about the old lady. A cop shows up and she tells him, "There's a man and a woman having sex right there!" She points out the window to the apartment a few blocks away. The cop shakes his head, "Sorry, lady, I can't see a thing." "Of course not, you fool," she says. "Here, use my binoculars."

It took 16 years, but the Forces of Righteousness finally got what they wanted in the "Meese Report," a skewered, un-scientific boatload of drivel which didn't bother with balance, facts or comparative research. The panel was stacked with anti-porn stalwarts, and—lo! And behold!— *they* found (after exactly one weekend immersing themselves in violent porn) that in their studied opinion, staring at S&M porn turns you mentally into a rapist. Is that true? It was, to *them*. Ignore the fact that porn in Japan has prevalent bondage and humiliation elements—and that Japan's per capita incidence of rape is one-sixteenth that of the U.S. Ignore the fact that in countries which are politically repressive—South Africa, the former Soviet Union, Uganda, Iran—sexual repression AND the incidence of sex crimes is higher. Forget that stuff. Raise the banner high and make sure the local 7-Eleven won't carry *Hustler* or *Swank*, that'll fix society.

Sigh.

So what does all this have to do with the interviews you're about to read? Everything and nothing. You're about to hear from sex soldiers who've been in the trenches, not history teachers in a West Point classroom, or some be-medaled general who's never heard the ricochet of a bullet. It's the same reality, viewed from a lower angle. The working stiff (pardon the expression) in a Detroit auto factory, assuming there are any left, can tell you what it's like to bolt a chassis or attach a door to a frame; the *Car & Driver* reviewer will tell you what's slick about the design and what stinks; the megabucks corporate owner will pontificate on why his cars are better than that other company's, even though they get lousy mileage and blow up when bumped in the fender. In the end, it's the same car.

There's near-universal righteous condemnation of the exploitive end of it, and lord knows it exists. Anyone want to defend using 13 year olds in Ukrainian porn videos? Do I hear any argument that it's the makers, not the performers, who make the big money? In our so-cool pseudo-enlightened age, does anybody truly believe you can ever leave the stigma of performing hardcore sex on camera behind you?

From my days as a men's magazine editor, I know a lady who's living a classically *Ozzie & Harriet* life in a lovely two-story house in rural Pennsylvania; two kids from a previous marriage, a doting, clueless second husband, and constant custody warfare with her ex-husband. She lives in dread that he'll find out about her hardcore porn past.

There's the saga of "Melissa Scott," a modern-day James M. Cain tale: a buxom porn model with the generic name "Barbie Bridges" cozies up to aged, learned but batshit-crazy evangelist Gene Scott, marrying him before he kicks off—then takes over his high-visibility video pulpit, faking her way through his TV ministry, trying to obscure her past as a spread-beaver model and porn producer, and the winner of the justly-obscure "Miss Nude CanAm Exotic" title in 1994. Praise the Lord.

Outsiders think making porn films is sexy. Outsiders think making movies in general is sexy. The guys who wrote this book seem to think so, based on their questions; their faces pressed to the candy-store window. Personally I've never found it a turn-on to watch strangers fuck. Having been on a number of porn sets, with a camera crew, lights, and the pressure to perform, I can say safely that the room will quickly smell like an old sock. On screen, the women are temporary representatives of Sex: they are (thank you, Charlie Sheen) goddesses. Off-screen, they're not a lot different from someone who sells real estate, or flies a plane, or keeps bees, or works at a supermarket.

That reminds me of seeing a porn actress I knew in my local grocery one afternoon in 1985. I recognized her; she didn't recognize me. To her, I had been one of a number of now-forgotten strangers she met one afternoon a year before. How would she know, why would she care, that I was there as the writer? It had certainly made no difference to her job. She was lithe, slim-breasted with a round, Susan Dey smile. I knew she raised horses, and in that area of the San Fernando Valley, there were still pockets of rusticity.

That was one of the few times I was on set for the duration of a shoot. I'd written two (or was it three?) scripts for a producer named Hal Freeman, to be shot back to back with overlapping casts and locations. This girl—let's call her Andi—did not show up on time the day she was booked. And really, as it turned out, there was no reason for her to have had an 8 a.m. call time, since her sole scene wasn't slated until late in the day—which was when she showed up. Oh, did I mention there was a brief eruption of outrage from Hal when it came to the actual sex scene with Andi? "What?!? She's got her fucking period?!?! Oh, for Christ's sake!"

In the supermarket, she didn't recognize me in the market aisle, and I didn't say hi.

On that same shoot, Hal asked me to accompany him and his cameraman to eyeball a potential location, an isolated suburban ranch house north of Los Angeles, in "Canyon Country." Prior to leaving, Hal had a morning meeting with some kid who had decided he'd try X-rated films. "He's supposed to have a twelve inch cock," Hal explained. The kid, who looked maybe 19 and seemed like he just breezed in from a Wisconsin 4-H club, showed up promptly with a chaperone, a pal who looked like Kato Kaelin: short, dirty-blond, surfer-cut hair, and puzzled. The Kid himself was tall, well-proportioned, but lordy mama, he had a face like Howdy Doody - pale, with wide, staring, blue eyes, too-thick lips, a broad nose, and freckles. Thankfully, exposing his potential stardom was not part of the audition.

"We're doing some charmin' cheapies," explained Hal, using his euphemism for his low-end features. "Three days total, we'll use you for two. You ever done pictures?"

The Kid galumphed an affirmative. "Well, yeah, I posed for pictures like that."

"No, no, pictures, movies," Hal countered, "Acting. Wait. Hang on. You mean you posed for pictures with your dick in your hand? With a boner?"

The Kid grinned stupidly. "Yeah, just…well, y'know…"

"Lissen, I'm gonna give you the straight shit. Don't do that. Don't go posin' with your dick in your hand. Y'know who looks at them pictures? Fags look at them pictures. You want fags t'look atcha?"

Howdy Doody's eyes went wide in ingenuous horror. "Well—no!"

"Okay, then don't do that. I'm lookin' out for ya. Monday and Tuesday, two-fifty a day. Okay, see ya. The girl'll give you the scripts."

We drove out to the semi-boonies and surveyed the location. It was nice but nothing grand, set on about five acres of land and shielded by trees. The camouflage would be useful. Private property or not, out of Los Angeles County or not, it was still considered illegal to shoot porn in California. The house had a swimming pool, clean rooms, an exhausted orange grove out back, and a hillside. Looking through one of the rear windows, I was struck by a vision of classic Americana and called Hal's attention to it. This small hill rose up in the back yard, with a white fence running along its ridge. Atop the hill was a single, lovely apple tree. Beside the tree a horse stood grazing. "Look," I exclaimed. "That's a set-up like a William Cameron Menzies design, like *Gone with the Wind*, or *Invaders from Mars* or something!"

"Unh-huh, beautiful," grunted Hal. "Nice production value."

The bearded, Falstaffian owner of the house offered leadingly that he was heavy into swinging. Oh, yuck! The images THAT conjured! He showed us around his barn and riding corral. He owned a half-dozen horses. "Oh, *this* is production value!" exclaimed Hal. "This is great. Y'know that scene where you got the older woman seducing the young kid in a warehouse? Rewrite that to a riding scene. He's the new stable boy. We'll use that new kid. She can ride the horse around the corral! *That's* production value! Then they can do a roll in the hay. Roll in the hay, get it? This is great!" Fine, scratch out "Warehouse," write in "Stable." At least in those days, porn films actually pretended to have scripts.

Hal was jazzed, but when we returned to his office, he went into a funk. His cameraman Rick—who went on to "real" movies and prefers not bringing up the 50 or 60 porn films he shot—asked what was wrong. "It's that new kid. What do I do with him? Who the hell do I know who can take a twelve-inch cock?" Frowning, Hal thumbed his Rolodex, then beamed. "Ah! Kim!"

(I'd met Kim, alias Sheri St. Clair, on my only previous set visit, also for Freeman. I thought she was pleasant enough, but inwardly smirked when she told me she was just doing porn temporarily; that she was saving her money and planned to go into real estate. Unh-huh, yeah, right, good luck. And as it turned out, she didn't. She opened a restaurant instead. So there. Shows what I know.)

Hal dialed the number. Understand: I heard only his side of the conversation. "Hey, Kim, Hal Freeman. How're ya doin'? Unh-huh. Huh. Really? Uh. Hey, we're shootin' some charmin' cheapies Monday, Tuesday, Wednesday, you free? Ah, heh-heh, no, not free, you get paid. Haw-haw. Okay, great. Okay, just two questions for ya. So, uh…can you handle a twelve-inch cock?"

Hal listened seriously, nodding, smiling once or twice, and nodding again. Then: "Okay, great. And the other question: uhhh…do you like horses?"

He had no idea how funny that sounded.

Hal's cameraman, Kim the restaurateur and erstwhile equestrian, my friend in Pennsylvania, the "Reverend" Melissa Scott—they're not alone in wanting to distance themselves from their pro porn experiences. For every Jenna Jameson or Asia Carrera who achieves some sort of financial success and stability, there are a thousand of dabblers who get into the racket for a few months or even a couple years, then leave for their own sanity. Has any performer ever crossed over from porn to "real movies"? Traci Lords is the only minor exception, and she's one out of, what, ten thousand? Would any legitimate casting director ever seriously consider Ron Jeremy for a lead character role in a major film? I happen to think he's a terrific performer, but professionally he's the eternal outsider, a novelty act.

In one pro-con speaking engagement, Jeremy tossed off the real-life drawbacks of fucking on film: it's there forever, and if you can't handle that, don't do it. That advice is all well and good if you're talking to someone with a healthy self-image who does not happen to have the stupid innocence of youth. But we're all invulnerable and eternal at 18 or 20. We know we'll never die - either that, or we'll never make it through 30 summers, never mind an ancient 40, and who gives a shit in the meantime? But people *do* survive, and the Internet is forever. "Gee, Billy, I saw a video last night of a girl who looks like your mom, but she had this Nigerian's arm halfway up her butthole! She took like eight jizzshots, and one gross guy who looked like Gene Simmons shot a load of choad right in her eye! Pinkeye, man! I downloaded it. We oughta show your dad!"

More common is the arc of Serena Robinson. She'd been doing hard-core for a year or two as Penny Morgan, Penney Morgan, Pennny Morgan, Penny Moore (people who type credits for porn films never were the best spellers), Ryan Thomas, and Ingrid Elliot (what's in a name?), with a willingness for anal scenes and a vivacious on-screen enthusiasm. A boob job and minor rhinoplasty made her quite a dish as the new, improved "Rachel Ryan." She got a couple days' work on a "real movie," *Clean and Sober*, as a nude corpse, thus beginning an affair with genuine movie star Michael Keaton. Whether it was a revelation of her past Keaton could not psychologically handle (Oh, come on. How long before you meet someone new do you ask, "So, what do you do for a living?"), or the sudden avalanche of tabloid publicity they received, or maybe even pressure on Keaton from studio and industry bigwigs ("Look, you fucking idiot, you think anybody's going to gamble twenty million bucks on a movie with you to end up with a film that's banned by every uptight religious mob in the country because you like fuckin' some slut in the ass? Come back when you sober up, meathead!"), the pairing collapsed. She returned to sphincter-widening porn, but soon landed another "legit" husband, actor Richard Mulligan, best known as the doddering geezer on *Soap* and the befuddled director in Blake Edwards' *S.O.B.* He was 60, she was all of 31. That ended acrimoniously two years later. I don't know what she's doing now. She was a good actress.

Suicides like Savannah, Cal Jammer and Shauna Grant, reprehensible AIDS-spreading like that attributed to Mark Wallice…it happens. It seems so much dirtier and cheaper than if the principals had been in the aluminum siding business, or upholstery. Is the rate of human tragedy in the porn biz any higher than other sub-section of humanity? Probably not, but it makes good TV tabloid gossip.

In the end, money talks. All those porn clips and films you can download off the net? The corporate carrier happily takes the dough from the porno suppliers. The 'net would not proliferate with the thousands of sex-surfing sites if the heads of AT&T, Comcast, and the rest refused to take pornographers' money. "We're not directly involved," they'll say. "Our customers have the right to do whatever they want on their bandwidth." Sounds like a pimp's excuse to a cop. "Hey, I jus' told her go earn some bread, I didn't say she oughta rent her snatch." I think pimps probably have the moral edge over telecommunication companies. Come to think of it, I've never been financially screwed by pornographers, but I can't say the same thing about legitimate movie, TV or magazine deals.

In dipping my toes into the waters of "adult entertainment," for good or ill, my name is linked with a couple notable landmarks. My name is listed as one of the editors on the infamous *Hustler* issue with the Dewar's ad parody suggesting that Jerry Falwell's first sex experience was with his mother in the outhouse (though I can't take credit for the ad. I wish I could!); heaven knows that caused a little stir—like a Supreme Court decision on parody. *The Adult Video News* cited Hal Freeman's couples-movie *X Factor* as one of the top 100 adult films of all time (I wrote it in three days). The same producer's goofy and raunchy *Caught from Behind Part 2* is misattributed to me and my then-partner; it was this film for which Freeman was busted for "pimping" under a screwy California law equating film-making with pandering, and his final appeal established another legal precedent, the statutory difference between hiring someone to perform and hiring them to screw you. That opened the floodgates to make LA's San Fernando Valley the world center of adult productions. Much later on, I wrote a silly softcore rock/spy spoof called *Sapphire Girls*, which co-starred the vivacious Mary Carey, fresh off her narrow loss in the race for Governor of California. Pity she lost; she would've been more fun than Schwarzenegger, as you can tell from her interview here. And as a character actor (they never ask me to do a love scene, dammit), I've acted in a dozen bikini comedies for my friend Fred Olen Ray, appearing with a couple of the many bimbos linked to Tiger Woods' high-profile sex scandals. Ah—brushes with greatness.

It's an alternate universe, where DPs, Viagra and jizz shots are as common as lube jobs, making change from a twenty, or mowing the lawn. Are the denizens any more outlandish or outspoken than people you know? Here are ten glimpses into that world- you decide.

Ted Newsom is a former editor of Hustler *magazine who has also worked as a screenwriter for adult films.*

INTRODUCTION
by Andrew J. Rausch

LIKE MOST BOYS, I discovered pornography at a fairly young age. First came the *Penthouse* and *Hustler* magazines, which introduced me to a world I could never even have imagined existed. Then, later, came the discovery of X-rated movies. I had a friend whose parents collected porn films. They had an extensive VHS library that they had illegally reproduced from rental copies, and man, they had just about every type of porn one could possibly imagine. They had movies with men and women having sex, women having sex with one another, women having sex with animals, and even one about a man who had sex with a mermaid. Being about 12 at the time, my friend and I were fascinated by these lurid little films. We had never seen anything like them. We tried to watch as many of them as we could, and soon they replaced badly-dubbed kung-fu movies as our main staple of entertainment.

And from that seed came a lifelong—I won't say obsession, because that's not quite right—*fascination* with X-rated movies. In the beginning, perhaps I was mostly just interested in seeing people have sex onscreen, but I soon found myself even more interested in what was going on *behind* the cameras. I found myself wondering what motivated the actors and actresses in these films. Did they actually enjoy what they were doing, or were their actions motivated by a monetary necessity? What were porn sets like? What kinds of budgets did it take to make these films? What kinds of things, if any, did porn stars refuse to do? What kinds of things went through their heads as they lay there moaning? Were all those stories about the "fluffers" true? How did adult film stars see themselves and their occupation? Was it true that most porn stars had troubled childhoods and had been victims of sexual abuse? Did porn stars have sex with their fans? What were the personal sex lives of porn stars really like? Did they even enjoy sex anymore, or did it eventually become a part of their work that they tried to limit to the office? Hell, I even wondered who came up with those silly parody titles like *Rambone* and *Saving Ryan's Privates*.

Eventually I grew out of watching porn films, but I never really got over my curiosities regarding the adult film industry itself. I thought I had, but I was wrong. When the film *Boogie Nights* came out, I found those old curiosities piqued once again. By this time I was well on my way to becoming an established film critic and author. I had written a number of books on the subject of mainstream cinema, including a book on the history of film. Another of those books was a collection of original interviews I had conducted with noted screenwriters like Steven Zaillian (*Schindler's List*) and directors like Robert Wise (*West Side Story*). Then one day it occurred to me that a similar collection of interviews with adult film stars might be interesting. Here was a way to learn and write about the adult film industry in a way that could be respectable.

My idea was a semi-academic book that could teach those who knew little about the subject (think *Porn for Dummies*) while still catering to those who were already fans by including many of the industry's biggest stars. My friend (and now co-author) Chris Watson and I had already come into contact with porn stars through a couple of low-budget "B" horror movies we had made. (Ron Jeremy had appeared in both *Zombiegeddon* and *Slaughter Party*, with Adam "Seymore Butts" Glasser playing a bad cop in the latter.) In short, the book seemed like it had potential, and it seemed like something that was doable.

I initially embarked upon the project by myself. I spoke to Ron Jeremy on the phone and pleaded with him to appear in the book, but he declined. He told me that he was working on his own book, and that he would only publish it if someone gave him a million dollars to do so. Then I met and befriended a porn star who wanted me to assist her in the writing of her own memoir. I flew to Los Angeles and stayed in her home for a night, only to be left locked out and stranded in a city I was unfamiliar with. One night everything was hunky-dory and we were talking about the potential of her book, and the next day she left me sitting there waiting for her. She didn't return my phone calls, and I never saw or heard from her again.

After hitting a few snags, I took a break and shelved the project for awhile. Then, when I eventually attempted to resurrect it, I found that I was working on too many projects to give it the kind of attention it needed. Embarrassingly, I even lost the tape of my interview with Taylor Wane. Realizing that something had to be done if I was ever going to finish this project, I reached out to Chris Watson and asked him to conduct the final four interviews needed to complete it. Thankfully Chris obliged, and the end result is the book you now hold in your hands.

For a while it looked like it would never be published. I had two agents who declined to represent it simply based on the description "interviews with porn stars," and we had more than a few publishers refuse to even look at the manuscript. The lesson here is that for all we may hear about how mainstream adult films have become, there is still a stigma around them that has yet to disappear. It may be somewhat less now than it was 20 years ago, but have no doubt it's still there.

Despite those hurdles, the book is now at long last being published. It is my hope that *Dirty Talk: Conversations with Porn Stars* accomplishes the things that I set out to accomplish. It was intended to provide an intelligent and impartial look at the world of porn films and the men and women who make them. I hope we have succeeded in doing these things while still providing a book that is entertaining for even the most hardcore (no pun intended) of fans.

Enjoy.

SEYMORE BUTTS

ADAM GLASSER, A.K.A. SEYMORE BUTTS, was born in the Bronx, New York, and later relocated to Los Angeles, California, where he attended Santa Monica High School. After graduation, Glasser owned and operated his own gym, where he also worked as a personal trainer. When Glasser experienced financial difficulties, he decided to rent out the gym for Hollywood film shoots in order to increase his revenue. One of the filmmakers who rented the space was an adult film producer who wanted to shoot a porn movie in the gym. Glasser observed the making of the adult film and soon realized that he was in the wrong business.

Shortly thereafter, Glasser borrowed a camera and directed his own adult film. He then edited it himself and made the rounds at a Las Vegas adult film convention, where he landed a distributor. With the sale of this first film, Glasser decided to become a full-time porn producer, director, and actor. He took on the name Seymore Butts, and with the help of his mother and cousin, established his own company, Seymore, Inc., which specialized in the "gonzo" style of pornography. (Gonzo is a genre of adult film that focuses less on the plots, dialogue, set design, and costumes of traditional porn.)

In 2001, Glasser found himself in hot water when he became the focus of an obscenity case in *People of the State of California vs. Adam Glasser*. The obscenity charges were leveled at Glasser after he made the film *Tampa Tushy Fest*, which featured a sexual act known as "fisting," which was up until then considered taboo by the American porn industry. Glasser later pleaded no contest to "creating a public nuisance" and was let off with a $1,000 fine. The court case made Glasser a star and resulted in the Showtime reality series *Family Business*, which focused on his life and career.

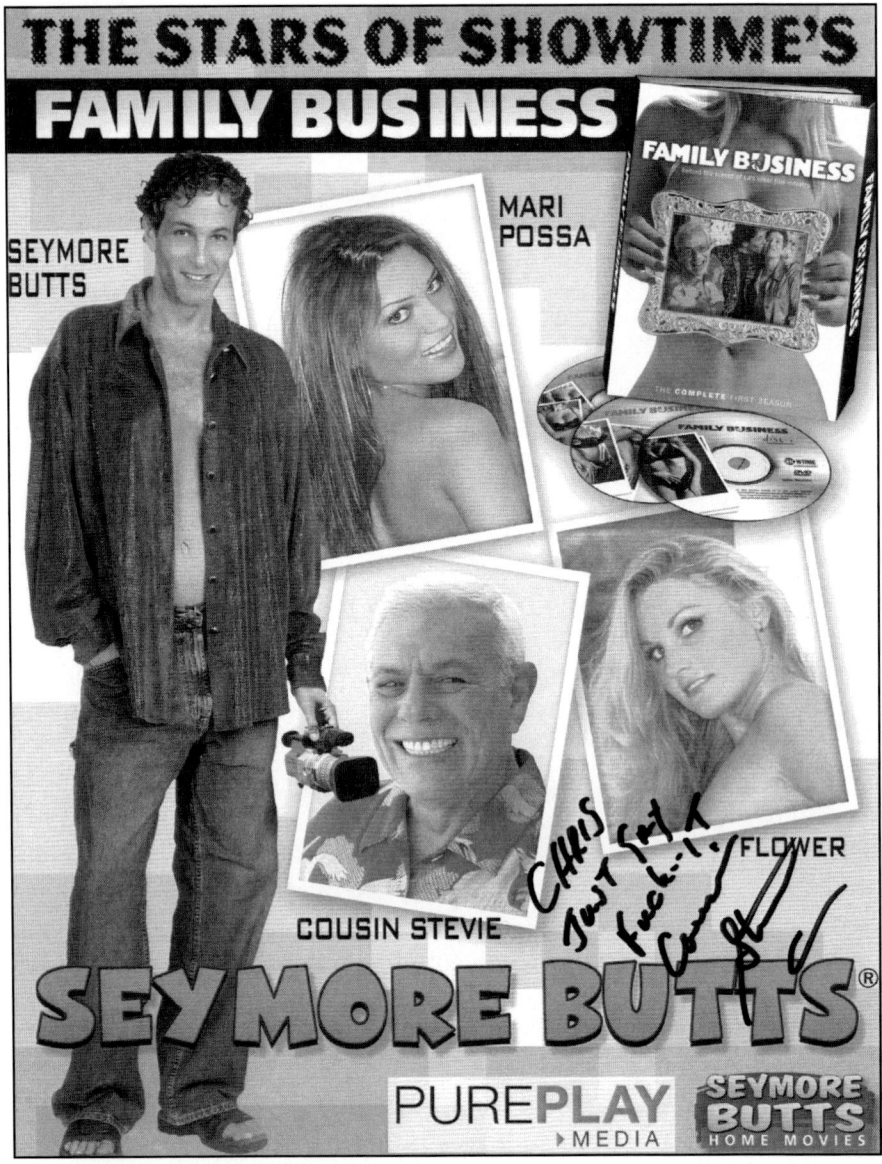

Seymore Butts is shown here with other stars from the television series
Family Business.

Glasser has directed more than one hundred adult films and has starred in almost as many.

KEY PORN TITLES: *Welcum to Casa Butts, Thighs Wide Open,* and *Seymore's Squirters.*

MAINSTREAM CRED: Seymore Butts was the focus of the Showtime reality series *Family Business*. He has also appeared in the no-budget Troma slasher film *Slaughter Party*, which also features porn star Ron Jeremy.

What kind of environment did you grow up in?

I was born in New York and raised right outside Riverdale in a nicer part of the Bronx. It was basically a middle class upbringing. We had a liberal Jewish family who told dirty jokes at the dinner table… My parents would take us to "R" rated movies if it wasn't anything too extreme. I lived in a big apartment building, which was part of a twin set of buildings. There were always kids around, and always companions to play with.

I got interested in girls early. I think I had my first kiss when I was eight. We moved to California when I was twelve.

How old were you when you lost your virginity?

I was fourteen, and I was dating a girl who was in junior high. Her parents both worked, so her house was empty after school each day. We cut school a little bit early one day to ensure that we had extra time. I think we both knew we were going to be doing it that day… The one thing I remember most clearly is that I started to hyperventilate before my clothes even came off. I tried really hard to control it, because I didn't want her to notice it, but I couldn't. Well, as it turned out, I didn't have to control it for too long because the whole lovemaking episode only lasted about three strokes and then it was over! [Laughs.] I had never even masturbated before that, so that was the first time I'd ever had an orgasm. That blew my mind. I didn't really understand what was happening.

What was your sex life like prior to your working in the adult film industry?

Very adventurous. While my peers were studying science and geometry in high school, I was studying female anatomy.

What initially attracted you to porn?

The opportunity to do something that seemed like it could be fun and profitable at the same time.

I've heard lots of guys talk about getting into porn just to have sex with a lot of women. Do you think that's a pretty naïve outlook?

Assuming they were actually able to get into the industry, it wouldn't be naïve for a guy to think that getting laid would be easier. But it's getting into the industry that's the difficult part. I myself don't necessarily take advantage of those things, but if a guy came into the industry with that mindset hoping to take advantage of those things, then I think it would be very easy for him to do so.

Your mother and your cousin Stevie help operate your company. How did they become involved with your business?

My mom and dad divorced after thirty-five years of marriage. My mom was faced with the prospect of having to go out and look for a job, so I hired her. My cousin was a salesman in the computer industry. The profit margins fell out during a certain period during the mid-nineties, and he was faced with having to find work elsewhere. I had an opening here, and, *voila*!

Has your mother ever seen any of your work?

She hasn't seen any of my movies, but she has seen porn movies, so she says. I haven't delved any deeper there. [Laughs.]

How did the rest of your family react to the news that you were working in the adult film industry?

I think pretty much the same way my immediate family did. If there were any negative comments made, I wasn't privy to them; they would have had to have been made behind my back.

You attended your high school reunion last year, and a lot of your classmates learned for the first time that you were a porn star. What was that experience like?

I was extremely nervous about that beforehand, but once I got there, I found that it wasn't necessary to be nervous. Everybody was very accepting, and very positive. Those who knew were extremely positive, as were those who were just finding out for the first time. It all turned out to be much ado about nothing, because I worried about it a lot more than I'd needed to.

What's it like the first time you have sex in front of the camera and a group of strangers?

I can only talk about it from a male perspective, but it's an extremely difficult process. It was easier for me than it is for the general population of actors working in the industry, because I was able to control the situation; I wasn't only the performer, but I was also the director, the producer, and the guy doing all the hiring, whereas in most cases I'm telling guys who they're going to have sex with. Most guys don't have that choice. I myself am more about allowing the girls to choose rather than the guy.

That being said, it's a very intimidating experience. Most guys fail at it the very first time they try.

You've been labeled the "King of Gonzo Porn." What exactly does the term "gonzo porn" mean to you?

Gonzo basically just means the movies are unscripted and reality-based with some form of interaction happening either between the camera and performers directly or the cameraman and the performers directly. That's basically the definition of gonzo in a nutshell.

What do you feel sets your films apart from those of your competitors?

I think I pay a lot of attention to detail. Because of my experiences and the length of time I've been in the industry, as well as the mainstream exposure that I've garnered, I have the opportunity to work with girls that others don't. That makes my movies special in a way. My movies are all about people having fun doing things that they really want to do. That's my basic formula, and I don't think others really prescribe to that concept. There's a lot of hostile-type filmmaking going on out there, but I tend to stay away from that.

What are your thoughts on those bigger-budget glossy films by companies like Vivid?

To put it bluntly, I think they're hard to masturbate to. They look too glossy, and too staged.

Tell me about the film Tampa Tushy Fest.

Well, to me it's just another one of my movies. Unfortunately, I was prosecuted for it on the grounds of obscenity, because there happens to be one particular sex act in that movie which differs from any of the others. Other than that, it's just a travelogue of a trip I take to Tampa, Florida, with my then-girlfriend Alisha Klass to do a series of promotional appearances.

It just so happened that Alisha hit it off with another girl who was on the trip. And that particular girl, Chloe, happened to be into this particular sexual activity known as "fisting." I was kind of interested in this, because I had never shot it before in my career. I was curious, and I asked her what got her into this. She explained that she'd been injured as a child, and, as a result, her clitoris is numb, so she can't have orgasms from oral sex or clitoral stimulation. Over time, she's developed a need to have large objects inserted into her vagina in order for her to achieve an orgasm. The hand seems to do the trick for her; especially a female's hand. So Alisha became quite curious, and the next thing you know, she's elbow-deep into Chloe.

Later, I reviewed the footage during editing... I was warned by a lawyer at the time not to release it, but I thought to myself, how could I not release it? I mean, this is a small portion of the film, and the obscenity law is supposed to look at the movie in its entirety. Aside from that, these women are having multiple orgasms during this particular act. I just felt this was very defendable. How can you say something's obscene that's causing someone to have such a pleasurable reaction? So I released it, and two years later—this was two weeks after President Bush was confirmed into office—my offices were raided, and I was prosecuted.

Was this the first time that act had ever appeared in an adult film?

That was the first time it had ever been released in a mainstream film as opposed to some mom-and-pop operation selling off someone's website. That was the first time it had appeared in a mainstream film in the 20 year history of porn. But I have to stress again that I didn't release it for the shock value. I didn't even advertise the fact that this act was in the movie, nor did I put any pictures of it on the video box. I just released it and then kind of let things happen as they may. For a while there, I thought I was clear.

That act was one which appeared on the so-called Cambria List. What exactly is the Cambria List?

That's the equivalent to the "seven deadly words" on radio. It's a list drawn up by a First Amendment lawyer who is very involved with the industry and some of its major players. He drew up this list for his clients of what he felt were safe acts to portray and what things were no-nos. That list was subsequently circulated throughout the industry.

What are some of the other acts deemed objectionable on that list?

Surprisingly enough, interracial sex is one of the objectionable acts listed there. Then, of course, there are the more obvious things like fisting, urination, defecation, and rape scenarios.

These are strange times in our country in that there's currently a very restrictive conservative social climate, and yet porn has become more accepted by the mainstream than ever before. Why do you think that is?

I think America is a hypocrisy in itself, so why shouldn't that follow the same hypocritical theme? [Laughs.] We're the land of the free, yet we have people trying to legislate our morality; what goes on in our bedrooms, what we watch on television, what we listen to. When everything else is that way, why shouldn't the view on porn be hypocritical, too?

Some people might say that you are in essence a pimp because you make money from women having sex. How would you respond to that?

I don't think I've ever been called a pimp before, but I see it as being a clear difference. First of all, I'm hiring women to do a job which is legal in the state of California. I'm paying them, and I don't take a percentage of their money the way a pimp would, although I'm certainly making money off the end product. I mean, what's the difference between me doing that and someone hiring a hot girl to do a diet pill advertisement? The only reason she's hired is because she's hot, and the guy knows he's going to sell more pills because of that. Everybody is exploiting sex to sell things. We just happen to offer the real deal, whereas most people are offering simulated sex.

MARY CAREY

MARY CAREY WAS BORN MARY ELLEN COOK on June 15, 1980, in Cleveland, Ohio. Born to two mentally handicapped parents, she was raised by her grandparents. When she was seven-years-old, she began studying ballet and dance. She made her stage debut at the age of 12 in a Miami City Ballet performance of *The Nutcracker*. The young girl's talent soon became apparent and she was offered dance scholarships to a number of prestigious schools. In 1998, she graduated from the Pine Crest School, which is a private Ft. Lauderdale preparatory school. The following year she joined the dance team at Florida Atlantic University. Taking the stage name "Mary Carey" because of her passing resemblance to singer Mariah Carey, she started working as an erotic dancer at the age of 19. Enticed by big money and dreams of stardom, she then went into the adult film industry. Carey quickly became a star, appearing on numerous television and radio shows, as well as appearing in a number of men's magazines.

In 2003, shortly after signing a contract with Kick Ass Pictures, Carey stepped into the national spotlight when she decided to run for governor in the California recall election. A number of other celebrities ran, as well, including Gary Coleman, the comedian Gallagher, and the eventual winner, Arnold Schwarzenegger. Running on a 10-point platform which included a proposed "porn for pistols" program, Republican Mary Carey finished 10th in a pool of 135 candidates. Carey later ran for lieutenant governor of California in 2006 and was even invited to a G.O.P. Fundraiser that included dinner with President George Bush. Carey was ultimately forced to drop out of the election due to personal problems, but has hinted that she would like to run for President of the United States one day.

A publicity photograph of adult actress Mary Carey.
Photograph courtesy of Dreamstime.

Tired of watching other people make money off her work, Carey established her own Mary Carey Productions in 2007.

KEY PORN TITLES: *Totally Mary, Cash & Carey,* and *Mary Carey Gets Carried Away.*

MAINSTREAM CRED: Mary Carey ran for governor of California and has appeared on numerous television shows, including a season on VH1's *Celebrity Rehab.* She has also appeared in the feature films *Being Ron Jeremy* and *Pervert!*

What kind of environment did you grow up in?

I grew up with my grandparents. They were very strict, but I was never unhappy. It never made me rebellious or anything like that. I was in ballet, and I was content just doing my ballet each day after school; I would be dancing from 4 p.m. to 10 or 11 at night with ballet classes. Then I would go home and do my homework and talk on the phone with my friends. I was very happy. They were strict, but I didn't mind. I wasn't angry that they were strict—I was glad they were.

Were they supportive of you as a child?

Oh, yes, very supportive. They gave me so much attention, and they spoiled me rotten! That's part of the problem… I'm a spoiled brat. [Laughs.]

Were you always an exhibitionist?

I was always putting on a show, dancing around the house. I would move the chairs and make my grandma and grandpa sit down and watch my dance routines. I loved that. I was always doing shows for them. Then at school, I was always the center of attention.

How old were you when you lost your virginity to a male and to a female respectively?

I was seventeen when I lost my virginity to a male. When I was sixteen, I almost had sex for the first time. We were going to have sex, but we didn't have a condom. I remember saying, "You don't have a condom?" So I didn't have sex with him. Then, when I was seventeen, I did it with my boyfriend. It was on Valentine's Day. He put rose petals on the bed and stuff... [Laughs.] But I was drunk, so I don't remember it very well.

My first time with a female was on camera when I was twenty-one. I really didn't know what I was doing.

When did you begin working as an exotic dancer?

When I was nineteen. I was on my college dance team and going to college full time. I needed a part-time job where I could make good money without having to work a lot. Then I found this job where I could work only sixteen hours a week and still make $400. It was called the Girl's House, and all I had to do was shower, and work out, and chat with people online. It was really easy and a lot of fun. Then some of the girls told me I should be a dancer, so I tried stripping, and I won an amateur contest. I stripped for five months. I loved it, because it was a lot of money, but it wasn't a whole lot of work. I loved being onstage. I like having a whole crowd looking at me. It was like getting paid to party, you know? I would drink, and meet people, and just have fun.

There are some people in the porn industry who say they're happy but don't really seem to be. It seems like a façade. You, on the other hand, seem like you're actually happy. Would that be a fair assessment?

I'm pretty happy. I mean, part of me wishes I'd never done porn. I wouldn't be where I am right now if I hadn't done it, but I do not like the way people judge you when you work in porn. I don't like the repercussions of being a porn star—when you date guys, they judge you differently. As an experiment, I'd like to meet a guy who didn't know who I was and not tell him that I'm a porn star to see if he'd treat me differently.

What are some of the problems with being a porn star?

Since you're a porn star, guys don't always take you seriously. Even though I only do girl-girl movies, people think you're a total slut and have sex with everyone. Also, I think that they don't trust you. And then there are the bad connotations with porn: they assume you had a bad childhood or were abused sexually.

What was it about the porn industry that initially attracted you?

I had always wanted to be famous, and I always liked going out and having guys tell me I was really pretty, and being the center of attention. So I liked that being a porn star meant that you were kind of a sex symbol to people. At least that was what I thought then—that people would look up to you as someone who was really beautiful. Now I realize that a lot of people just think porn stars are sluts. But, at the time, I liked the idea of being every man's fantasy. I always felt like everyone was looking at me when I went out in public already, so I might as well make money off that. I wanted to be famous. I wanted to be like Jenna Jameson. That was my goal when I got into porn.

How did your family react to the news that you were working in porn?

I was married at the time, and it was weird when my husband's family found out. All of a sudden, they thought I was a horrible person, and they didn't like me anymore. They didn't know for a while, but now they thought I was bad. I tried to explain to them, "You loved me, and you thought I was a great girl, and I was doing it then. I'm the same person—the exact same person. My career—what I do for a living—doesn't change the person I am."

The hardest part was with my sister-in-law. We'd kept my working in porn a secret, but obviously when I ran for governor, we couldn't keep it a secret any longer. Well, when I ran for governor, her friends at her high school saw me on TV and said, "Oh my God, isn't that your sister-in-law?" Then, because of that, the girls at school didn't want to be her friend anymore. And then the guys started harassing her. All of those bad things happened to her because of me; because I was a porn star. That was the most difficult thing for me. I felt very bad for her having to go through that because of me.

My grandmother was senile when I was doing it, so she didn't know. And then my mother is very proud of me. I don't think my mom fully understands what porno is, but she supports me. I've done some soft-core movies, which are available at Blockbuster, that are rated R. She rents those and tells everyone at Blockbuster that I'm her daughter. She also wears "Mary Carey for Governor" shirts around. My mom is just so proud of me. She wants me to be more famous. She loves it when we're out and people recognize me. That gets her so excited.

How often does that happen?

Sometimes I get recognized a lot. If I'm in full makeup, I get recognized constantly. If I'm not in makeup, I don't get recognized as much.

Once I was at the airport, and no one said anything. Then another time I was at the airport, and three different people approached me one right after the other.

Now people are recognizing me without makeup because of a show I did on the Playboy Channel called *Totally Busted*. For that I wear almost no makeup. They're setting people up for practical jokes, so they don't want me to look too good and be too made-up or then people will figure out that something's going on. Since I don't wear much makeup on that, people are starting to recognize me without makeup.

One time when I was in Houston, Texas, I had the funniest thing happen to me. I was eating at a restaurant, and the waiter comes up to me and says, "You know, you look like a younger version of Mary Carey." And I said, "I am Mary Carey, and I'm only twenty-three!" [Laughs.] And then, before I knew it, every single waiter in the place was at my table asking me to sign pieces of paper and napkins.

About a year ago, I was in Ft. Lauderdale. My girlfriend and I were walking down the beach, and someone started yelling out of their car window, "Mary Carey!" That was strange to me that they recognized me. If I was someone else and I saw me walking down the street in Ft. Lauderdale, I wouldn't really believe it was me. I'd be like, "Why would she be walking down the street in Ft. Lauderdale?"

When I shoot *Totally Busted* in L.A., there will be times where I'll be out shooting on the street corners and stuff, and a lot of people notice. Fire trucks will drive by and stop, and they'll take pictures of me. That was the kind of attention I always wanted. Sometimes when I get annoyed with it, I remind myself that that's what I always wanted; I wanted to be recognized everywhere I went.

What was it like the first time you had sex in front of a camera and a room full of people?

It wasn't really that strange when I first started. The first person I ever had sex in front of a camera with was my husband; we had done a sex scene for our website. There were only two or three people there, but it was more difficult with my husband than with the people I didn't know. That sounds strange, right? You'd think it would be like doing something that's normally a personal thing in front of a group of people, but when you're doing a movie it doesn't feel so personal.

It's strange now, because I usually work with the same crew, and these people have become my friends. It's really hard because they're my friends... I mean, one minute I'm joking around with them, and the next they're watching me have sex. But then I always remember that they do that everyday, so they're not even fazed by it.

A lot of people see porn as being the same thing as prostitution. How would you respond to that?

When I first heard that I thought, 'What are they talking about? That's not true!' But now, as I've been in the industry longer, I do think it is kind of similar. After all, you are getting paid to have sex. The difference is that both people are getting paid. With prostitution, you would generally be paid by the person having sex with you, where in the movie you have the director paying you both. I think in that way it's different. I do think it's very similar, but at the same time, I like to say it's different, because I don't consider myself a prostitute.

But there are adult stars now who do actually prostitute. There are a lot of them that do that. There's a website where you can go to and see the porn stars who are actually hookers. I kind of wish porn stars wouldn't hook… I mean, the appeal of a porn star is supposed to be that you're unattainable; that you're a fantasy girl. If you can have a porn star for $1,500, it kind of takes that away.

You'll see some of these porn stars arguing that making films is different from being a prostitute, yet they're out there prostituting, so obviously in their heads, it's the same.

Have you ever had sex with a fan?

Not really. I mean, there was a guy I had sex with who also happened to be a fan, but we didn't get together because he was a fan. He's a friend, and he was a big fan of mine. I met him at a *Penthouse* photo shoot a few years ago in Miami. We became friends, and a year later, we ended up having sex once. But I don't really have sex with fans. I have a friend who does the escort thing, and she has sex with fans all the time.

You seem to meet a lot of famous people. For instance, you recently partied with Dr. Dre, and I know you've met a number of NBA players. Do you get hit on by many celebrities?

I do get hit on by celebrities when I go out, which is really funny. Some of them don't know who I am, and some of them do. With some of them who don't know who I am, they just think I'm a pretty girl. Then when they find out who I am, they don't want to hang out with me; they're scared that it's going to reflect upon their image. I remember one of the guys from the Black Eyed Peas came up to me once and said, "Aren't you Mary Carey?"

With the basketball players, some of them knew who I was, and some of them didn't. But they just seem to like me. Another cool guy I met was Shaquille O'Neal's cousin. We're really good friends now. I was at a Miami Heat game, and the security guy came over to me and said, "Shaquille O'Neal's cousin wants to meet you." So I gave him my number, and he flew my girlfriend and me out to the NBA All-Star Game last weekend. That was great. I got to meet Tracy McGrady… I have a thing for NBA basketball players. I think it's because I'm really tall. I love basketball. I love the players. I'm just obsessed with basketball. My dream is to have sex with an entire NBA team. Isn't that horrible? [Laughs.] I don't want them to rape me, though. I'd like it to be the Pistons, or the Lakers, or the Heat, or the Rockets… I also like the Raptors. I like all those teams.

Dr. Dre was awesome. My friend Klaus is his bodyguard, and he got me to hang out with Dr. Dre once. Dre is just a really nice guy. He's so sweet, and he's such a gentleman. He's kind of quiet; just a really nice guy. I didn't have sex with him, unfortunately. [Laughs.] You know, he's married. But he was fun to hang out with. He told me I was a fun girl. Too bad he's married!

What aspects of working in porn do you enjoy most?

I love the conventions and meeting fans. I love being in front of the camera and taking pictures. I love all that. I love it.

What aspects of working in porn do you enjoy least?

I don't like that there's a risk of disease. It's scary that you're doing a job where there's a risk that you could get herpes, or HIV, or chlamydia. Even with the testing… You know, it's not one-hundred percent effective. I dislike that. I dislike some of the movies that get a little bit too extreme. I've seen some girls who are a mess mentally because of some of the movies they've done.

You made a now-infamous appearance on Howard Stern's show where you wound up with your head in a toilet bowl. How did that happen?

I'd already been on the show once with my mom and my grandmother. So I was trying to think of an idea to get back on the show again, because every time I went on, I would make more money dancing and get more hits on my website. So then I took an IQ test on the show. Then I agreed to put my head in a toilet bowl the next time. That was great, because the bowl was clean, and I didn't really get my head into the toilet. I mean, my face didn't get wet or anything. As long as I acted like it did for the show, they didn't mind. I kind of dipped my hair in the water a little so it looked like it. It was fun. I've been on the show five times now.

How did you end up running for governor of California?

The owner of Kick Ass Pictures, which is the company I'm under contract with, called me up and said, "Do you want to run for governor?" And I said, "That sounds like a good idea." [Laughs.] That's how I ran for governor.

How much of that was serious and how much was a publicity stunt?

It was all done for publicity. That was the whole purpose, but the key to making it funny was to pretend that I was serious.

What were some of the highlights of that time for you?

I loved appearing on all the news shows. I did *The O'Reilly Factor, Heartlands, Scarborough Country*, the CNN shows… I went on *The Tonight Show*. I did a game show with some of the other candidates, and I won that. I won $21,000. That was cool. I had a great time.

Do you feel that the media treated you differently than they did the other candidates?

If anything, the media gave me more attention than a lot of the candidates. I'd say I probably got more attention than anyone else, other than Arnold Schwarzenegger. They were very nice to me. I think they were surprised that I could actually form sentences! [Laughs.] They just thought I was going to be a stupid bimbo or something.

When you were interviewed about your campaign on Hannity and Colmes, *you flirted quite a bit with Alan Colmes. As Mr. Colmes is not exactly what one might call a handsome man, I was wondering, were you legitimately attracted to him or were you just playing to the cameras?*

I love Alan Colmes. He has such a great personality. I don't always like the guys that other girls think are cute. I like the guys who have a great personality. I have a personality fetish, I guess.

Obviously, running for governor gave you a lot more exposure. How did that change your life and your career?

Running for governor has definitely changed a lot of things. My appearance rate at strip clubs has gone up a lot, because more people come to see me now. The movie sales have increased dramatically. My website is better, and it gets more visitors. I get recognized in public a *lot* more. But then, that could also be because I was still kind of new in porn before that, and now I've been working longer, which has made me more visible. A lot of very cool things have happened for me as a result of running for governor. I made an appearance on VH1. I made a Russ Meyer-type indie film called *Pervert!*, and I got my Screen Actors Guild card for that. Now there may be a new reality series about me, and it's all because I ran for governor. That experience allowed me to show a mainstream audience my personality.

Who are some people working in the adult film industry that you admire?

Definitely Jenna Jameson, because she sort of paved the way for the rest of us, and she made porn more mainstream. If it hadn't been for her, I probably wouldn't have known anything about porn stars. Sharon Mitchell is another person I really respect. Now she's running AIM (Adult Industry Medical), and she's really helped the industry a lot. I admire Larry Flynt, because of his stand for freedom of speech. Those are all people who made it possible for people like me to be successful in this industry.

What's your sex life like offscreen?

Well, I was married until this past October, so it wasn't really that exciting. You know, it was just me and my husband, and I wasn't really that attracted to him after a while. I get bored having sex with the same person, and after a while, I don't really want to have sex with them anymore.

But now that I'm single, it's been pretty crazy! I guess I'm a bit of a slut. [Laughs.] I like a lot of different guys, and that's my problem. I like a guy, I get really horny, and then I want to have sex with him right away. I keep thinking, I've got to hold out and be less slutty, but then I can't. I just get too horny.

What's the craziest thing you've ever done off screen?

I don't know. Just having sex with a lot of different people is crazy to me, but I haven't really done anything too outrageous. I don't do anal sex, and I'm not really into rough sex. I have a lot of sex with a lot of people. Like I said, my fantasy is to have sex with a whole NBA team. That would just be crazy.

Are you interested in women sexually when you're not working?

When I first started working, I wanted to do the girl-girl thing a lot more. But then I realized that I'm not really into girls like that. I enjoy looking at girls naked more than men, but I really enjoy sex with guys more.

Do you prefer sex with porn stars or regular guys?

I like sex with regular guys. To me, porn guys are kind of gross because they're having sex everyday with a different girl. That kind of freaks me out, so I like regular guys. The only problem is that most regular guys cum really, really fast, and I don't like that. Porn guys last a long time. Some guys get scared to have sex with me because they think I'll be disappointed because they can't last as long as porn guys.

A lot of people debate about whether or not porn films are art. What is your take on that?

I think they can be. I think some porn films are art and others are just people having sex. I mean, if it's a movie where a girl is doing double anal, I don't think you can really call that art. I think that's…gross. But if it's a pretty movie with a plot, I think that's a kind of art in itself. It's funny that people argue about porn being art; I doubt many people look at a beautiful painting and jerk off. People are, however, doing that to porn, so I don't think porn is being made to be an art form.

As you mentioned, a lot of guys are going to be out there masturbating to these films. Does that turn you on? Is that something you think about when you're making a film?

You know, I never really think about that. Now I'm going to be thinking about it… [Laughs.]

What are some advantages and disadvantages of working with a small company like Kick Ass Pictures as opposed to one of the bigger companies?

I chose to go under contract at Kick Ass Pictures, because I wanted to be the big fish in a small pond. Because they're a smaller company, they give me more attention. Had I gone with a bigger company, I never would have run for governor. I might have been popular, but I wouldn't have become a household name the way I have with Kick Ass Pictures.

As far as disadvantages, I guess the main one would have to be that they can't pay as much as some of the bigger companies. The movies don't have big budgets, and I don't think the distribution is all that great. I get a percentage of all the movies that are sold, but if the distribution isn't that great, you're not going to sell as many copies. And they're not quite as well known as some of the other companies, but I myself have managed to become quite well known. I think I'm more well known than most of the Vivid girls, so I don't mind. I like being the only girl under contract there, because they spend more time with me, and that's nice.

You've managed to become somewhat of a big name despite the fact that you make relatively few films. How have you managed to do that?

Obviously, running for governor played a big part in that. I also think it's because I've done a lot of girl-girl movies and only a few boy-girl movies. Then people wanted to see the boy-girl movies more, because there weren't many of them. Then it's kind of like a new thing. I think that's definitely helped. I also think my personality has been a big reason for my success. I think you can tell what my personality is like in the movies. Most porn girls are really loud, and I'm really friendly, and silly, and goofy. I don't take myself seriously, and I think people can see that in the movies. I think that makes me stand out more than some other girls.

Financially speaking, how do you get by making less than ten films a year when there are girls out there who are literally working everyday?

Because I'm under contract I get a salary. Well, I guess I don't get a salary anymore… Before I ran for governor, I got a $6,000 a month salary, which was $72,000 a year just to do six movies, which really made it something like $6,000 per scene if you think about it. Most of those other girls only get something like $800 a sex scene. But now I get seventy-five percent of the profits from the movie sales.

The movies are nice because they get my name out there, but I make most of my money from the appearances I make. My website also makes me quite a bit of money.

When you're making a film, how many of your reactions are genuine, and how many are acting?

I think all of my reactions are real when I'm doing boy-girl, but when I'm doing girl-girl, it's one-hundred percent acting, because I'm not really that interested in girls. I do like having sex with girls. It does feel good, but I don't enjoy it as much.

What kinds of mistakes do you see girls making when they first break into the industry?

This is an easy question to answer. The biggest mistake I see girls making is not knowing anything about the industry or how it works. They just want to make money, so they do double anal or something like that in their first movie. Once you do that, they expect you to do that all the time. Some girls do everything right away, and then fans become tired of them because they have nothing new to offer, and then their careers are over.

ASIA CARRERA

ASIA CARRERA (real name Jessica Steinhauser) is not your typical porn starlet by any stretch of the imagination. She has a 157 IQ and is a member of Mensa (a group comprised of the most intelligent people from many different nations). By all accounts, Carrera's childhood was a difficult one. The product of Japanese and German immigrants, Carrera was pushed by her parents—perhaps beyond the breaking point—to succeed. "I was not an especially motivated child," Carrera has said. "I was an overachiever only through genetics and incredible pressure from my parents. They wanted me to go to Harvard and be a doctor or a lawyer, and I wanted to play piano and hang out with my friends." This pressure involved routine and severe beatings for "poor" grades such as Bs. Carrera's high school career was an impressive one; she was a New Jersey state spelling bee champion, a National Geography Olympiad winner, and had already held two classical piano concerts at Carnegie Hall by the time she was fourteen.

However, the pressures placed on her by her parents would ultimately cause her to become such a perfectionist that she could no longer see her successes as successes. "I feel like I'm useless and can't do anything, when in truth, there's nothing that I can't do," she has said. "I aced every subject at school but was never the best. I got 1440 on my SATs, but I met someone who did better, and I felt like crap. Every time I find out that I'm not the best at something, I don't want to do it anymore." At age sixteen, the situation with her parents worsened, and she ran away from home. She then taught colloquial English at Tsuruga College in Japan as part of an academic exchange program. She soon landed a full academic scholarship to Rutgers University, where she majored in Japanese and Economics. During this period she also worked as a nightclub dancer, often working seven days a week.

Asia Carrera

Asia Carrera wrote, directed, and or appeared in more than 250 films before
retiring in 2003. Photo courtesy of Asia Carrera.

At age 20, Carrera appeared in a nude layout in *Club* magazine. She
then sought out and found a career in porn. Shortly thereafter, she appeared in *Playboy* magazine under her real name, Jessica Bennett. In
late 1993, Carrera inked an eight-picture deal with Vivid Entertainment.
She quickly became one of the biggest adult film stars of the 1990s. In
1994, she received a record-breaking ten AVN nominations and was also

named Female Performer of the Year. Carrera then became an internet trailblazer, becoming one of the first adult film stars to operate her own website. After leaving Vivid, she began writing, directing, and starring in her own films, beginning with *A Is for Asia*, which remains her most popular film. She then crafted one of the most ambitious and artistic porn films ever produced with the avant-garde *Apassionada*, in which she also played classical piano throughout.

An avid *Wall Street Journal* reader and somewhat of an investment guru, Carrera invested most of her earnings and accumulated a nest egg that allowed her to retire from porn in 2003 at the age of 30, after having appeared in more than 250 films.

KEY PORN TITLES: *A Is for Asia, Apassionada,* and *Search for the Snow Leopard.*

MAINSTREAM CRED: Carrera worked as a body double for Jennifer Tilly in the film *Fast Sofa* and also makes a cameo in Joel and Ethan Coen's *The Big Lebowski*.

Tell me about your childhood.

I grew up in an extremely strict household. Both of my parents were immigrants, and both of them had done extremely well academically. They met at NYU while my father was getting his doctorate and my mother was getting her degree. So, of course, they expected me and my siblings—I'm the youngest of four—to go the academic route. I did very well in school, because I was pushed so hard, but it was extremely stressful. I was a very unhappy kid; I tried to kill myself, and I tried running away from home a lot. Basically, it was just too much pressure to put on a child.

So, I finally ran away from home for good when I was sixteen years old. I lived on my own for a while, then got found out and was placed in a foster home. I spent the last half of my senior year there. Then, when I turned eighteen, I ran away from there, and I spent some time doing some things I didn't want to do so I'd have a place to sleep and food. That was when I learned how to separate sex and love. Then, that fall, I started at Rutgers University on a full academic scholarship. When I got to Rutgers, my priorities were a bit skewed. I wasn't bent on getting an education; I was bent on making money. So I took advantage of my scholarship and worked as a stripper seven days a week and saved up all my money until they kicked me out of school.

In the past you've described yourself as having been "an ugly child." How old were you when that started to change and you started to be noticed by boys?

I was the only Asian kid in my school, so that was why everyone made fun of me. I thought I was funny looking and unattractive. Once I got into high school where there was a bit more diversity, then I guess it was okay to be me. Once I was in college, that was when everyone started to say I was pretty. And then I got my nose done when I was eighteen, and that gave me self-confidence. When I was little, the kids called me "big nose."

I understand you got arrested immediately after losing your virginity. What happened?

I was fourteen years old, and there was this kid in my biology class that I thought was absolutely gorgeous. He passed me a note that said, "I'm gonna come and pick you up tomorrow night at three o'clock in the morning." And I said okay. He was only sixteen, and he wasn't old enough to drive yet, so he had to steal his mom's car to do it. So I met him outside my house, and we went and parked behind an indoor tennis facility. We had sex. It was very fast, and then the cops came and found us in the parking lot. They arrested us, took us to the police station, and called our parents. [Laughs.] That was my first time, and my parents were alerted, and it did not go over well.

In fact, it was such a bad experience that I didn't even try anything like that again for another two and a half years.

There's a misconception that women somehow get trapped into doing porn. However, you made the decision yourself and sought out a career in the adult film industry on your own.

I've always said that porn was a godsend for me. It was the best opportunity that I could have been given at the place where I was in my life. Because I was set on making money, it was the place to go. I was given money. I was given opportunities. They treated me like a star. I had the chance to do acting, writing, directing, producing… I learned how to author DVDs. I learned how to run my own website. I just took advantage of the opportunities I was given in every possible way. I made the most of it, and it turned out to be a very positive thing for me. I got a great kick out of it. I was paid so well that I could take most of my time off and just sit at home with my computers and work on my website.

It just really worked out well for me. For the girls who just want to work to make drug money, it's not going to work out so well. [Laughs.]

What was it like the first time you had sex in front of a camera and a room full of people?

I remember being very nervous. I just wanted to do a good job. I had my eyes closed the whole time, so I wouldn't see people. [Laughs again.] If you look at any of my early scenes from the first year, you'll see that my eyes were closed the whole time so I could just feel like I was one-on-one with the other person and just ignore the room around me. But I've always got my ears open, listening to the director and what he's saying. I try to look on camera like I'm having a good time, but in my mind, I'm trying to be professional and give the director the angles he wants; give the lighting guys the angles that they need. There are so many people on set that you need to please besides the person you're working with that you can't actually be as into it as the audience would like to think you are.

I understand you got cheated financially on your first film. What happened?

They made me do eight people for $800! They stuck me in a couple of orgy scenes. My first scene was a three-way, my second scene was a three-way, and then there were two orgy scenes. That was all on my first day! It was just a whole lot of sex for $800. I had no idea how much work they were gonna have me do, and it was my first day, so I didn't know any better. And I've never let them hear the end of it. It was directors at Vivid. I've worked with them a lot since then and even married one of them (Bud Lee), so I made sure they heard about it for the rest of their careers!

Did that change your perception of the industry?

No, I just took it as a learning experience. After that, I made sure I always checked with my husband-to-be ahead of time. You know, how many scenes was this going to be, who was I going to be working with? I didn't know how the first time to get a breakdown ahead of time of what exactly was going to be involved. After that, I knew to always ask ahead of time.

Why did you continue to work with Vivid after that?

They were the best in the business. They had the really beautiful girls, the highest quality movies, and they had directors I really liked. It all worked out really well. I would definitely recommend going the Vivid route, if you can, right away.

How did your family react to the news that you were working in the adult film industry?

I don't really know. After running away at seventeen, I never called home to ask.

You have a well-documented anxiety of being around strangers. Has this ever affected your work?

It made my job extremely difficult. [Laughs.] People have no idea how difficult it was for me to just get up out of bed each day to go to work. I thought about getting on Paxil or one of those drugs, but then I was afraid that it might take away any special spark of charisma that I had. I really relied heavily on my makeup and wardrobe as my Dumbo's magic feather; it made me believe I could do it and become that character. I would hide behind that. But at the end of the day, it was such a relief when I could just wash it all off and put on my combat boots and jeans and go back to being a grubby nerdy kid.

In speaking with you, it's immediately apparent that you are extremely intelligent. Is it difficult for you to relate to other people in the industry?

[Sighs.] I never really fit in. The girls would come to me for advice on things, but I never really hung out with any of them. They would basically treat me about the same as the other kids in school had. They were only nice when they wanted something from me. When I was in school, the kids wanted to copy off my papers. When I got into porn, it was, "Hey, Asia, can you help me set up my own website?" or "Can you help me with this?" [Laughs.] I didn't mind, though. It's all right. I'm used to being the nerd or the geek who doesn't quite fit in.

Is there a lot of in-fighting within the industry, or is there a sort of camaraderie?

There are some girls who find it competitive, but for the most part, all of the girls just approach it like it's a big slumber party. I mean, there's enough work for everybody. There's no reason to be catty.

There was one very big-named girl in the business who was always very mean to me, and I never understood why. [Laughs.] Her book just came out if that's any help…

Jenna Jameson.

Yeah, she was always very catty to me and I could never understand why. But usually that's not the case. Normally everyone's just buddy-buddy.

Most people grow tired of doing whatever it is they do for a living. Do porn stars grow tired of sex?

There are girls who come in and do what I did, which was, in my first six months I made seventy-five movies. And yeah, you will get burned out doing that. You can't keep that kind of pace up.

Does that being tired of sex carry over into your personal life?

I was single at the time, and a lot of porn stars are for that very reason. Most of the guys are single so that they can give their best efforts to the camera and not at home. Once I slowed down my production of movies, it no longer affected my sex life at home. Then I was only doing one or two movies a month. If you only do that many movies, it's no big deal. It's only like two or three sex scenes a month. That leaves you with more energy for home, and home is always better. You're always looking forward to sex at home.

Like most porn stars today, you've had some plastic surgery done. Has it become a necessity to have plastic surgery done in order to continue working in the porn industry?

No. Not at all. The directors and producers would have you believe that they prefer natural. To some extent they do, because there's a big market for the young innocent-looking eighteen-year-olds. So, when you come in, you should start out with that natural look. Do that for about two years, and then start getting surgery. Then, as your look changes, you'll get work again and again and again. It keeps you looking fresh for the cameras. "Oh, she got boobs! Let's hire her." Then it's "Now her boobs are bigger! Let's hire her again!" It keeps you going.

Tell me about Apassionada.

That's my buttkicking piano movie. That was my baby. I spent two years shopping that one around, trying to find a company that would finance it. I wrote, directed, and produced it. It was semi-autobiographical. I played classical piano all the way through it. It received seven AVN Award nominations that year. Then, several years later, I worked from nine to five in an office with Simon Wolf authoring the DVD for *Apassionada*. I was part of the three-man team that made the DVD, which received nominations for Best DVD and Best DVD Extras.

That was one of quite a few films you directed within a two year period. Do you have any plans to direct again?

No. Unfortunately, I can't stand directing talent in this business. They're so flaky! [Laughs.] They're not motivated. They're not ambitious. They don't care to learn their dialogue. They mess up the lines that I write! It's all very frustrating for a perfectionist like me.

Do many fans ask you for sexual advice?

They ask me for a lot of advice, but you'd be surprised how little of it is sexual in nature. Of course, there are the old standbys, like "How do you not get in-grown hairs?" and "What's your favorite position?" [Laughs.] That's about all I hear in regard to sex.

People ask me for advice about how to raise their kids so they won't turn to porn. They ask me for computer advice. I get lots of computer questions and questions about running a website. It's a strange gamut of things. I think it has to do with being Asian in this society. It's interesting all the things they ask about that are not sex related.

What's the dumbest question you've ever been asked in an interview?

"What are you doing after the interview?" I've had some interviewers ask some stupid questions like that, hoping they're gonna get lucky.

That was actually my next question.

[Laughs.] Really?

No, of course not. I'm just joking. So that question never works?

No. The only one who got lucky was Don, my husband. He asked me some really good questions, and we became friends after that. I went to his website and looked him up, and I said, "Man, you're really cute!" [Laughs.] And the rest is history; we were married a year ago.

On your website, you list frequently asked questions. What's the most annoying question that you're asked frequently?

"How'd you get started in the business?" That one's annoying just because it takes so long to answer, and I've had to answer it so many times.

There's a rock band named after you now. What are your thoughts on that?

I think it's flattering, but I really don't know much about them. They contacted my husband and asked if I minded that they used my name, and I thought that was really cool. But I haven't heard anything that they've done yet. They're supposedly working on a song with my husband right now, but I don't know much about them.

Have you ever had sex with a fan?

Well, I dated a British guy for five years who was a crew member in the business. The first time I went over to his house, he had an eight-by-ten photo of me hanging on the wall that I had signed for a "friend" of his. He'd kept it, and there it was hanging on his wall. Does that count? That's about the closest I've ever come.

Usually the only time I meet fans is at the convention, and there's always a big line of them; like a thousand people. That's not really conducive to taking someone home.

Have you had any bad experiences with fans? I would imagine in your line of work you get people who are fixated on you.

I've had some stalkers. I've had a few people who made me feel really uncomfortable. I showed up in one state and was signing autographs, and someone sent flowers up to my hotel room, which was booked under my real name. That made me feel freaky, like the guy was downstairs waiting for me or something... He swore to me later that he wasn't, but it made me feel really scared in my hotel room. I've had people who called my house who sat outside in their cars. I had one guy who sent a mass mailing out to all the adult video companies and told the secretaries, "There's some cash in it for you if you can hook me up with Asia Carrera's home address and phone number." One of the companies forwarded that to me, and that was pretty scary.

You haven't had anyone break into your house or anything like that?

No, but I've had the cable installers looking around and suddenly realize whose house it is that they're in. Then they come back every couple of weeks to ask if my cable's okay!

There don't seem to be many "A" girls who are Asian. Is the industry discriminatory, and have you personally had any encounters with that?

The Asian girls who are in the business tell me that they look up to me for breaking down the barrier. I was the first Asian girl to be put under contract and the first Asian girl to become "A-list." I'm proud of that, but I think it was because I'm only half-Asian. I think I softened the features enough that they could pass me off as being a sexy brunette if they needed to.

I have found prejudice in the magazines. You're not gonna find me on the cover of any magazine other than *Oriental Dolls* or *Oriental Women*. That kind of pisses me off.

Now that you've broken that barrier, do you see the industry getting better in regards to prejudice toward Asians?

As soon as I left Vivid, they signed another Asian girl. Then when she left, they signed another Asian girl. I guess that's doing well for them. But I still haven't seen any of the magazines put an Asian girl on the cover. *Penthouse* magazine specifically tends to avoid Asians like the plague. I've shot for them twice, but never as a *Penthouse* pet. I posted a message on my website and told everyone to send *Penthouse* an e-mail and tell them that they wanted to see me as a pet. That made *Penthouse* angry. They threw a fit. They were like, "We're not racist. We're not prejudiced." Then, given that they have a lead time of about six months, there miraculously appeared their first Asian centerfold six or seven months later. It wasn't me, but it was quite a coincidence.

Have you been asked to do many things in films that have made you say, "No, I'm not going to do this"?

Yeah, sure. Like the gangbang stuff. That stuff just doesn't interest me. I don't do anything I'm not comfortable with. That includes scenes with two guys. I did that for a little while at the beginning of my career, and I just decided I wasn't comfortable with that, and I didn't want to do that anymore. I want to look like I'm really enjoying myself on camera. If I'm not, I'm not, and then it ceases to be fun.

I've read that you've only had anal sex on film three times in the two-hundred-and-fifty-plus movies you've done. Is that something you're uncomfortable doing, and if so, what was it about those three projects that were different?

Well, I had just left Vivid Video. I had just walked on my contract, and they were calling all the companies and telling them not to hire me. I was sure that I was never going to work again, so I decided I needed to do something. What am I going to do? So I took some money out of my bank account and decided to make my own movie, which was *A Is for Asia*. In that film, I did my first ever anal scene, my first ever scenes with toys, my first ever facial cum shots. That film went out the door at number one, and it established me as a big star even though I'd left Vivid. It was kind of like my smug "Ha!" to Vivid after they'd tried pulling that nasty stunt on me. [Laughs.]

A Is for Asia is still my bestselling movie to date, and I own all the rights to it. It still makes me a lot of money.

The other two anal scenes I did were for friends of mine, Tommy Byron and Randy West, who both paid me very well for them.

What kind of advice would you give to a female considering a career in porn?

Pace yourself. Don't do everything on the first day. If you do a gang-bang on the first day, there's nothing left to do for an encore. You want to start out maybe just doing girl-girl stuff if you can get away with it, and then step it up every six months to a year. That also gives the audience something fresh to see, and the directors a new reason to hire you. Save your plastic surgery for at least two years. And the biggest thing I would say is that you definitely need to save your money. This is a job that usually only lasts until you're thirty. If you wake up and you're thirty and you haven't saved a penny, you're gonna be in big trouble.

What kind of advice would you give to a male considering a career in porn?

Go get a real job! [Laughs.] It's not a great job for a guy. They don't really make enough money to save and invest. They don't get any of the glory. They don't do signing tours or dance on the road. It's really thankless for the guys, and it's awfully hard work. If it wasn't for Viagra, three-quarters of the guys wouldn't even be here.

You've lent your voice to some adult anime films. What was that like?

That was really hard work. The anime stuff is pretty sick and twisted. [Laughs.] I spent three weeks screaming in agony at the top of my lungs and saying, "No, no, I can't take it anymore, arggghhh!" It just gets to you. I thought I was losing my mind, and I was glad when I stopped doing that. They don't allow mainstream porn over there in Japan, so they allow some pretty sick and twisted cartoon anime stuff. These films had the machines that screw the girls, and double or triple enemas and the girl's naked and holding it. It's just kind of sick and twisted.

You once expressed an interest in operating your own production company. Is that something you'd still like to do?

Well, I kind of did that there for a while. It was too much of a pain in the butt collecting my money. I would have problems with bootlegs in places like Australia and South Africa, and there was nothing I could do about it. Or there would be an account in Spain that wasn't paying me $2,000. The collecting is just a real pain in the ass. If you don't have a company following that stuff up full time, it's just not worth it.

As a rule, who's better at cunnilingus—men or women?

Definitely women. Women know what another woman likes. And I think men would probably be better at blowjobs if they could get over the whole blow each other part. [Laughs.]

Scenes from adult films are lifted and reedited into countless other films. When these scenes are reused, do you get repaid for that?

No, definitely not. In the past I've used my website as a soapbox to say, "Don't buy these films because I don't get paid for them." It sucks, because they use those scenes over and over again, and we never get paid again for them.

Sexually, what do you feel you're the best at?

Probably just the overall sex scene. The guys always seem to enjoy working with me so much that they cut their rates to work with me. They say it doesn't feel like a job when they're working with me, because I really enjoy what I do. I only work with the guys I really like, and I only do the things I like, so I am actually having a good time. It's not a chore to work with me. They always know that when they work with me, it's going to be fun.

Of which career achievement are you the most proud?

Probably my website. I've been called an internet pioneer, and I'm proud of that. It really introduced me to a whole new realm of fans who were computer-savvy geeks like me. It helped the world take me seriously. It showed people that I wasn't just a pretty face. My website is my baby. It's been my baby for the past eight years. It's my pride and joy.

Do you make quite a bit of money from your website?

I made more money when I first started because there wasn't so much competition. It was really nice when I first started. There wasn't anyone else out there who ran their own site. Well, I guess there really still aren't many who run their own sites… I wasn't competing with all the professional sites, either. It's definitely a good source of income, though. I've been retired for a year now. I also took a year off when there was the AIDS scare, and both times, I just relied upon the income from my website, and I was fine.

You stood in as Jennifer Tilly's body double in Fast Sofa. *What was that experience like?*

I had to go into the dressing room with her and take off my shirt and pull down my pants. She looked at me and she goes, "Arrghh! Okay! Fine. That's perfect!" [Laughs.] She was all embarrassed.

It was a really easy job. I just spent the day hanging out on the set with Jennifer Tilly and Eric Roberts. Eric Roberts was so cool. He was really down to earth. He just sat there and asked me questions about porn. Then, at the end of the day, he says, "You know what? I made a porno movie once." I said, "You're kidding," and he said, "Nope. I made it under the name 'Eric,' and my dad said it was going to be the end of my career." He was like, "It's all over now." But no one ever found out, so that's out there somewhere.

You also made a cameo The Big Lebowski. *What was that like?*

That was really cool, too. That was their first day of shooting, so they were still nervous. I was the only one who wasn't nervous, because they were shooting in a porn studio where we had shot all the time, and I was playing a porn star. I was completely at ease. They wrote some dialogue for me, so I could get my Screen Actors Guild card. That was really cool of them. It was a great experience. It was really easy. I said my lines, and then they said, "Okay, now take off your shirt and say your lines." So I did it again, and I heard that when they played back the dailies later they said, "Oh, my God! She says her dialogue exactly the same with her clothes on and with her clothes off!" [Laughs.] Wasn't that why they hired me? Then they all asked for autographed photographs afterward.

When people see you in public, do the clothes ever throw them off? What I mean is, do they ever stare at you like they know you from somewhere, but with the clothes on they just can't quite place you?

You should look on my website and see what I look like without makeup, because I look completely different. So the people who recognize me without makeup are ones who are really familiar with my website, and they've seen those pictures. I'll say, "How did you know?" And they'll say, "It was the combat boots" or "the flannel backpack"; little things they would only know from my website.

I can't go out with makeup on, though, or I get stopped everywhere I go. It's really awful. I very rarely ever wear makeup when I'm out unless I'm coming home from the set. I hate being recognized in public. It's embarrassing. I had a guy one time in the middle of a convenience store start yelling, "Oh, my God! It's Asia Carrera! Quick, sell me a camera so I can take a picture before she leaves!" And I was like, Oh, my God, please kill me now. [Laughs again.]

These are the kinds of stories we never hear about in the mainstream media: I understand you helped to fund an animal shelter?

Yeah, the Agora Hills Animal Shelter. I bought a dog run there, so the dogs could play outside. I also funded a kitty cat habitat, which is a sunshine-filled room where the cats play, and they have no cages. They've all got baskets, and toys, and a carpeted area where they can run around. It's really nice for the cats. It always made me cry whenever I'd go to a shelter and I'd see them in their little cages, so I funded a place where they had no cages for cats.

You recently retired from the adult film industry. What factors led to that decision?

Well, I always said I was going to retire at thirty, so I did. It's really that simple. I was just about to move to England to be with my boyfriend of the previous five years. Three weeks before I was supposed to leave, I met Don, and he convinced me to stay and marry him, and I did. So we got married three months later, and that was it. I decided to retire after that. We moved to Hawaii. Two months later, I got pregnant, and now I'm sitting here in Utah, nine months pregnant, and waiting patiently. I'm as big as a house. I'm looking forward to having the baby and probably never doing porn again.

You mentioned that your child is one of the reasons you don't want to return to porn, and I can certainly respect that. Are there many women working in the industry who have children?

Yeah, you'd be surprised. It's not something they talk about in interviews, but I would say that more than half the girls are mothers.

Do you have any regrets?

No, I never have any regrets about anything, because I'm happy with who I am and where I am. Every step along the way was just something else I needed to do to get to where I am today. It's all just part of a learning experience.

My last question: What the hell are you doing in Utah?

[Laughs.] That's a good question. And no, I'm not a Mormon. My husband, Don, has his warehouses here for the products he ships. He thought it might be nice to be closer and be able to oversee his business on a more day-to-day basis than he could from Hawaii. And when I saw the prices and property values here I said, "Whoo-hoo! That's the place we're going!" In LA and Hawaii, the prices are just out of control. This is also a quiet, safe place to raise kids.

NINA HARTLEY

NINA HARTLEY was born Marie Louise Hartman in Berkeley, California, in 1959. The youngest of four children, she attended Berkeley High School, where she developed an interest in the performing arts. One highlight of Hartley's time in the drama department was her crafting the toga worn by future Oscar-winner Timothy Hutton for a performance of Euripides' *The Bacchae*. While in high school, Hartley attended a screening of the X-rated John Holmes film *Autobiography of a Flea*. The film proved to be a revelation of sorts for Hartley, who was still a virgin at the time. Unsure of exactly how she would go about it, Hartley set her sights on a career in the adult film industry. In 1983, while attending nursing classes at San Francisco State University, she began moonlighting as an exotic dancer. (She would ultimately graduate *magna cum laude*.)

In 1984, while still working her way through college, Hartley was discovered by adult film star Juliet Anderson (a.k.a. Aunt Peg). She then made her adult film debut in the film *Educating Nina*, which became a hit. Several more Hartley vehicles followed that year (including the hit *Anal Annie and the Backdoor Wives*), establishing Hartley as a rising star in the world of adult entertainment. She has since gone on to appear in more than four hundred first-run adult films and (including compilations) appears in more than seven hundred films in all.

Alongside such adult stars as Ron Jeremy and Jenna Jameson, Hartley has helped to put a face on the adult film industry. She has appeared on many television programs and documentaries, including appearances on *Donahue*, *Oprah*, and *The Tyra Banks Show*. She has also appeared in mainstream music videos and appeared in a prominent role in Paul Thomas Anderson's 1997 film *Boogie Nights* alongside such heavyweights as Burt Reynolds, Mark Wahlberg, and William H. Macy. In addition to these accomplishments, Hartley has penned the book *Nina Hartley's Guide to Total Sex*.

Since making her adult film debut in 1984, Nina Hartley has appeared in hundreds of films and continues to work today.

KEY PORN TITLES: *Educating Nina, Splendor in the Ass,* and *Nina Loves Girls.*

MAINSTREAM CRED: Nina Hartley appears as William H. Macy's hilariously unfaithful wife in *Boogie Nights*. In addition, she has appeared on numerous television shows including *The Oprah Winfrey Show* and *The Tyra Banks Show*. She also appears in the Tupac Shakur music video "How Do You Want It?"

What was your childhood like?

I was born in 1959 to politically active parents who were politically on the left side of the spectrum. A couple of years before I was born, my father was blacklisted for being a communist. He lost his job, because he was actually a communist. I grew up in Berkeley, California, the youngest of four siblings. The first three were born within five years, and then five years later I was born. So there was a big gap in age between me and my siblings.

In some ways, my childhood was very idyllic and very liberal. We lived in the same town as my mother's mother and her sister. I saw my cousins regularly, I saw my grandmother and grandfather regularly... I had my own room. We had pets.

But I was also rather lonely as a child. The blacklisting had definitely put the whammy on my parents, and they had withdrawn from political life. So during my early childhood, their marriage had been thrown into chaos because of the abrupt loss of my father's job. We were then a one-income family with a female breadwinner, which was very unusual. My mother was a scientist, and she had a job with the state department of health. So we did okay—we owned our own home, had a backyard, the whole thing... But my parents' personal lives were affected greatly due to the loss of my father's job. He'd been a rising local media star, and that just changed everything. But I never knew any of that. I only knew my parents after all that had happened. So I was a bit lonely, and my parents were very other-directed toward saving their marriage and trying to figure out the meaning of their own lives, which was very popular to do in Berkeley during the sixties and seventies. And while I certainly went through a period of having my own issues with that, I now have a deep appreciation for what they did and what happened to them. They gave me the tools that I have now to assist me within my life and being good at what I do and being a good sex educator. I'm actually very glad for it. Sure, there was a time that I wasn't glad for it, but now I am very grateful. My parents are still living—they've been married sixty-one years—and I speak to them once or twice a week.

As a child, I loved to read. I loved to play in my tree house. I had a very best friend who moved away when I was eight, which was very sad. When I was ten, I got to go on a plane by myself all the way to Scotland and visit her for a whole summer. That was great. That was a lot of fun. And that year, while my siblings and I were all out of the house, my parents discovered Zen Buddhism and really got very deeply into it. They're still with the organization today, and they've been Zen Buddhists now for nearly forty years. My mother is an active priest, and my father is retired.

I got my first period when I was thirteen-and-a-half, just like the book said you do. And I found myself interested in sex early on, even though I wasn't seeing any of this. My parents didn't make out in front of us, and I didn't regularly see adults without clothes on. I was interested in naked bodies long before I'd ever seen one, or been exposed to anything like that. That's why I firmly believe that the basic nature of our sexuality is hardwired into us, just like our eye color and hair texture. So on one hand, while I may not have been trained in all these social niceties, I did have the freedom—because of the time, because of the place, because of my parents—to recognize and discover my sexuality for myself. And all the books supported my right to that. The feminist movement was quite new then, and it wasn't yet anti-porn. So in the early seventies, when I was going through puberty, all the books were saying to women, "Take responsibility for your orgasm. There's no Prince Charming. You get to have a sexual life. You can do it yourself. Learn about your body. Don't wait for him to somehow know more than you." Very empowering. Very good stuff. That was the era of consciousness-raising groups, where women would get together and examine their genitals in mirrors. Porn is everywhere now, so people have a hard time realizing how rare that was and how empowering that was for women to be told by other women, "Take a look—this is your body. Here's your clitoris, and here's how it works. It's okay, and it's not dirty." It was hugely revolutionary, and for someone who's my age, it seemed like common sense. I had no bad attitudes about my body to overcome, because I was coming to my sexuality at the same time this information was all around me in Berkeley. I was so grateful for it, because I never once felt for even a minute that I was weird because of my sexual desires. Again, I didn't have sex until I was eighteen. I started necking at parties at fourteen or fifteen. So we're talking twelve, thirteen, fourteen here… And I was just so grateful to have, instead of value judgments—being a slut or being immoral—I realized I was a bisexual person. I was an exhibitionist. I was a voyeur. So I discovered early on that there were words and descriptions for the feelings I had inside myself.

I was so grateful. I may have been socially awkward and not at all comfortable even being alone with a boy, but I was able to be comfortable with my ideas and my desires, because the book said it was okay. I'm thrilled beyond belief that I was not raised in a religious environment. I was not raised with parents who thought they could tell me what to do. They didn't hit me or anything like that. They may not have been as involved with my inner life as I might have liked since they were so distracted by their own, but they never ever gave me any denigrating words or attitudes about who I was. They didn't like what I ended up being, and they thought they had something to do with it. Finally a few years ago, I was able to tell them that the reason I'm in adult entertainment is not because they were or weren't there—it wasn't something they did—but it's because of who I am. I'm this kind of person. I'm exhibitionistic, I'm voyeuristic, I'm bisexual, I'm polyamorous. I'm not conventional in my sexuality. So for me, adult entertainment was great. It was really overall a wonderful thing for me to have found. And for that, I have my childhood to thank. If I had been raised in a different time or place, with the same sexuality, which is hardwired, I would have had much more conflict about it. I might not have ever made it to adult entertainment. I might have had to leave my church. I might have had to run away from home— all because of who I was—if I'd had different parents or been raised in a different place.

You once snuck into an adult theater as a teenager, and you've said that experience changed your life. Tell me about that.

I discovered written pornography at a used bookstore when I was about fourteen, and I was just instantly entranced. This was in Berkeley, and up on Telegraph Avenue there were also comic book stores, and I discovered underground comics. *The Freak Brothers… Harold the Hippie* was absolutely fantastic. And there was this one comic called *Young Lust*, which was a takeoff of the romance magazines. It had horrible art—really bad art—but one of the stories in it resonated with me. Again, I was reading all this stuff, and I was a virgin—I'd never seen a naked boy in real life. I'd seen the occasional photograph, or classical paintings, but I'd never actually seen a live naked boy. But I was reading these stories and saying to myself, "This is so cool. I want to do that when I grow up." I wanted to be confident and competent about sex and my body. I didn't know how that was going to happen, and I didn't know what someone did to become confident or competent, but I did know I wanted it. It was the seventies and we as women were told that you could have the life you wanted, and I wanted a life of relaxed sexual experimentation and a large group of friends with whom I could be naked and have fun. And I didn't want this to be problem to anybody. I understood, as a feminist, that I had both the right to my sexual life and the responsibility to do it in a sensible manner. Again, if I'd been raised in a different culture and had felt a lot of guilt about my sexual desire, I would have stuffed them back down inside myself and then gotten very desperate and lonely. Who knows what would have happened.

So I'd discovered written pornography, and *loved* it! And I was babysitting for this swinging seventies couple up the block with a waterbed and a padded frame, which was all very cool. And I discovered their bedside stories and loved those too. I also discovered two wonderful and incredibly important art books. One of them was *Erotic Art of the Masters*, and the other was *Erotic Art of the West*. You know, Rembrandt makes a damn fine dirty picture. [Laughs.] So here I learned that pornography could be not only fun and amusing, but it could also be considered art. And that just let me know that sex could be more than a laugh, a giggle, and a twitter. One of the books I found beside the bed was *Autobiography of a Flea*. So I read the book. And between home and school there was an adult theater—the Mitchell Brothers theater in Berkeley—and they were showing *Autobiography of a Flea*. I'd read the book, so I wanted to see the movie. You know, you've read *War and Peace*, let's go see Audrey Hepburn in *War and Peace*! It was summer, and I was almost eighteen, and I decided I was going to go check it out at the three-thirty showing after school one day. On the way in I'm thinking, please don't card me, please don't card me. I didn't have a fake I.D.—I wasn't trying to get into any other venues. And since this was Berkeley and the seventies, they didn't card me.

I was all alone, too. I didn't take anybody with me. I didn't tell anybody what I was doing. So I went into the theater, and when I got in there, I was thinking, please nobody sit next to me. And of course, a single young girl in an adult theater at that time acted like soap on greasy water—instantly I had a ten foot radius of privacy all around me. All of the men in the theater—all eight of them—moved away from me to the edges of the theater. I realize now that they were completely discombobulated by the appearance of a teenager in their midst. This was not a place for girls, but hey, I wanted to see the movie. And when the movie came on, I was just struck dumb and completely transfixed. I had not had sex yet, I had not touched a penis, I had not touched a vulva—I had not done anything sexually. I was just utterly transfixed. I just loved it. My joke is that my inner Cookie Monster came out and said, "Me want that!" I was already into dance; I was already into theater; I was already into performance. I didn't know how, why, or where, but I knew that for me, sex performance was absolutely where it was at. It was what I wanted to do. It combined everything that I wanted in life—naked people, performance, having sex with people without having to know them. Up until then I didn't even know this existed, but I knew then that this was what I wanted to do. It would be another eight years before I actually ended up making a movie, but I knew then that that was what I wanted to do. I didn't know if I would ever be able, and I had no idea how one did these things, but I did know that I wanted to do it.

In 1982, you went to work as an exotic dancer at the legendary Mitchell Brothers O'Farrell Theater.

That's pretty close. I actually started my dancing career in 1983, at a now-defunct theater called the Sutter Street Cinema in San Francisco. I did the amateur night there, and this was after years of wanting to strip… I didn't do my first stripping until I had convinced myself that I could be a feminist—a *real* feminist—and still take my clothes off on stage. I recognized then that if it was something that I wanted to do for me, then that was a feminist act, because it was me, as a woman, taking control of my life and doing what I wanted to do for myself. So I did the amateur night at Sutter Street Cinema, and I got the job—because I was clearly the only amateur! All of the other women showed up for the fifty bucks you got for entering, and they were clearly all professionals. It was also amateur photography night, so I knew there was going to be amateur photographers in the audience. I practiced, and I did a little routine with a little stupid cheesy vibrator for some penetration… I just went there and I had a good time, and I won, and I got a job. So I danced at the Sutter Street Cinema. I did a peep show one night a week, two or three sets a night, with another woman named Sunny. And that was a great introduction, since the audience was concealed behind mirrors. So I was having sex with a girl, which was one of the reasons I ultimately got into porn, because that was where the naked women were, and instead of an audience of men, it was a room of mirrors. I knew there were people behind the mirrors, but when I danced, all I was looking at was me. I learned how to dance and how to present myself as a performer. If I got really close, I could see through the mirrors and see guys behind there; sometimes they would be masturbating, which I thought was so cool. So I did that for about a year, and then I did amateur night at the O'Farrell Theater. And I danced there from 1984 until I graduated in 1985, and then I went into movies full time.

And then, in 1987, I started combining feature dancing with movies. And I stopped feature dancing in 2003, after doing that for fifteen years.

How did you make the transition from dancer to adult film star?

Well, I had wanted to make movies for a long time. My then-husband and I even met with an agent, who was just so creepy and icky. It was like, if I have to get into movies for him, then I guess I'm not going to do it. And then my husband met Juliet Anderson at a grocery store. He got her card, and we sent her some polaroids. And then she called me up. Once we found a way in, as any woman will tell you, it was then really simple to get in. She hired me and put me in *Educating Nina* in 1984 and acted as an agent and mentor for about a year. And then I was pretty much on my own. I didn't even get a proper agent for movies until last year. So for the first twenty-two years of my career, I was freelance. It was relatively easy... Once a woman finds a way in that she's comfortable with, it's easy. It's like Ron Jeremy says, "Men are paid because they're able, women are paid because they're willing."

What kind of advice did Juliet Anderson give you when you first came into the business?

She gave me the advice that I pretty much already knew, but she also gave me the support to follow through. Don't do anything you don't want to do, don't work with anyone you don't want to work with... She did try to get me to have a signed contract for each gig, but by then, that system was definitely dying. No one was going to sign a contract with you for a single movie. She said to hold out on my rate, make sure I got paid what I wanted to get paid, and to have a good time.

You've lamented in the past that video was coming into its own when you entered the business, so you never got to appear in a "big movie." Do you have any affection or affinity toward the adult films of the seventies and early-eighties?

I don't really. I wanted the experience of working on film because I know they tried to tell stories, and they had a more stately, relaxed way of shooting. But if you go back and look at those movies from the seventies, they are—for the most part—a dark and furry place. As pornography, where you can see everything, modern pornography works much better. What's nicer about the seventies movies is, generally speaking, most of the people in them were some kind of sex freak or other. Because back then, you didn't go to high school thinking, I'm going to be a porn star when I grow up. You found it because you were already a hippie, on the fringe, unusual, a free spirit, sexually open and adventurous... And that's how you found your way into porn.

So now, the biggest problem with video is that anybody can make a movie without needing to stop for a minute and think, do I really want to do this? And now they start out at a much younger age, when you're still young and stupid. At the age of twenty-one, we all do stupid things. I don't know about you, but I'm glad there was not a camera around for some of the things I did between eighteen and twenty-one. There were few eighteen year olds in porn in the seventies, other than Sharon Mitchell. So I don't have a particular affinity for the movies of the eighties. I liked a couple of them. One of the ones I watched that was very, very important to me in terms of me thinking, Wow, I want to do this, was made in 1980. And I recently went back and watched it, and as a movie, it worked well. But as porn, not so much. Again, dark and furry. So I know that people lament and decry the pubic hair styles of today, but pornography works better today as a visual medium, because the lighting is better, and because the hair around the genitals is trimmed and shaved. Today the performers are more sexual athletes than actors. Back in the seventies, you had to be an actor who could also have sex. These days, you are an athlete who has to say a few words. There are very few people today who can act and have sex.

Your views are rather progressive. You're a feminist, a Zen Buddhist, and a socialist. Do you ever find it difficult to relate to the other girls?

Well, these days with my age being what it is, I don't have to relate to them as peers or as friends. I'm more like a mentor. I'm old enough to be their mother. I'm friendly with them...I talk about their experiences and about work, but I don't talk to them about politics. They don't care about politics. These are people who, in some cases, were born after Ronald Reagan left office! So to them, political progressiveness is an odd thing—and so are things like sisterhood, solidarity, and feminism. And the people who I'm friendly with, we don't talk much about politics anyway. I know that I'm far to the left of everybody else in the business, and that's okay.

Certainly there have been some negative changes in the industry during the time you've worked. What are some of the more positive changes that you've seen?

Number one is that we now have the AIM Healthcare Foundation. So now we have a centralized place where everybody gets their HIV and STD tests once a month. We can go there for counseling. You can go there to get a shot to cure those STDs that can be cured by a shot. They have referrals for twelve step programs if anyone needs that. There are referrals for counseling for anyone who needs that. It's a community-based health clinic that does a wonderful job of keeping HIV out of the adult business. Since we started it eight years ago, there have been fewer than ten cases of HIV, and all of those cases—every one of them—happened because people did not apply common sense to the behaviors to which they agreed. On the website, we say just say no to cream pies. Just say double no to anal cream pies. Say no, no, no, no to double anal cream pies. Just say no. Some of these are stubborn young people who are invincible and think they're going to be beautiful and young forever, so all we can do is say we recommend highly that you do not do these things. And the times that HIV has come into the business, it has been because people said yes to very dangerous activity. So AIM has been a very positive thing.

A negative thing is that the bar to enter is lower, so you don't have to think about it for two seconds before you do it. This is a problem, because you do six movies, and then you want to leave… It probably won't come back to bite you in the butt, but it could because these films last forever. And when you're eighteen, you don't think about forever. When you're eighteen, you can't imagine being thirty. On the upside, more and more the stigma of having been in porn is lessening, although in many jurisdictions around the country, a woman's involvement in adult entertainment of any kind can get her kids taken away and can be used against her in a custody battle. But today, more than in the past, if you've done porn, you can still go on and do other things. That's a positive.

In 1993, you were arrested for performing an erotic show at an industry fundraiser. What happened, and what exactly is "felony lesbianism?"

Well, felony lesbianism was a tongue-in-cheek joke about one of the rules we had broken, which was, up until that point, a law against homosexual behavior. It was considered one of those infamous crimes against nature. We were charged with conspiracy to commit prostitution, solicitation of prostitution, appearing in an obscene or illegal or immoral performance, which pertained to the lesbian contact in the show. That law, I'm very happy to say, was completely overturned by the good people of Nevada. In fact, they turned that down in the very next voting cycle.

This was a fundraiser for the Free Speech Coalition.

That's kind of ironic that you were arrested for expressing yourself at a fundraiser for the Free Speech Coalition.

Of course. [Laughs.] And you had to find the store, go to the store, pay some money... There was not ever any danger of anyone just stumbling upon it. And the police were just there waiting. It turned out the organizer had been warned not to do this again, which was something he didn't tell us. So we did what it was that we did, and they arrested us. We ended up spending the night in jail. The first of us got out at about nine, and the last at about noon.

You had a fairly significant role in the film Boogie Nights. *Do you feel that the film accurately portrayed the adult film industry, or was this just Hollywood's notion of what it was like?*

Not really. It's a Hollywood movie about something. So if you're part of any professional subculture, and Hollywood makes a movie about you, you're going to see all the stuff they got wrong. They got a lot of the details right, but the business was illegal at that time, and they really made no effort to show that. Sets were being busted back then, etc. And John Holmes notwithstanding, the women are the stars of porn—not the men. The female characters in the film were a bit underdeveloped, I thought. And they left out part of my role which explained why my character was the way that she was, so [Paul Thomas Anderson] kept my character as more of a cartoon, I think. But there was dialogue that we recorded that filled the character out a little bit more than what appears in the finished product.

JILL KELLY

AFTER GRADUATING FROM HIGH SCHOOL, Jill Kelly (real name Adrianna Moore) began working as an exotic dancer. She soon befriended porn star Tiffany Million, with whom she attended the 1993 CES in Las Vegas. This opened Jill's eyes to the financial opportunities available in the porn industry. The following year, she began working in porn. Before settling on the moniker Jill Kelly, she appeared under a number of pseudonyms, including Adrian, Calista Jay, and Seth Damien. Rather than signing an exclusive contract with a production company, Kelly worked independently on a wide variety of films. This exposure soon made her one of the most popular and recognizable starlets working in the industry.

Shortly after she began working in porn, Kelly met and fell in love with porn star Cal Jammer. The two soon married, and both Kelly and Jammer retired from the business. Within a year, however, the two returned to work. Sadly, this happy union would soon become a tragic story, concluding with Jammer's reportedly committing suicide on Kelly's doorstep. Although few people knew Jammer's motives for taking his own life, Kelly was briefly treated as an outcast by the rest of the porn community, who initially blamed her for the tragedy.

Despite these setbacks, the goal-oriented Kelly would continue working and carving out a name for herself as one of the premiere porn stars of her time. Most polls ranked Kelly as the second biggest porn star of the 1990s, just behind Jenna Jameson. In 2000, *Club* magazine announced Kelly's selection by her peers as the Porn Star of the Millennium. The popular actress has also won a number of awards, including XRCO Performer of the Year, a handful of AVN (American Video News) Awards including Female Performer of the Year, and the 1999 Cannes Film Festival award for Best American Actress in an Adult Film. In 1999, Kelly achieved elite status in the industry when she was selected to appear in the compilation

Actress Jill Kelly was the second biggest adult film star of the 1990s and is
recognized as one of the greatest stars the genre has ever produced.
Photograph courtesy of Scott Shaw.

film *The Top 25 Adult Stars of All Time*. During her ten-year career in the adult film industry, Kelly appeared in more than 400 films.

KEY PORN TITLES: *Sorority Sex Kittens 3, Chasin' Pink,* and *Jenna's Built for Speed.*

MAINSTREAM CRED: Kelly has worked on a number of "B" movies (*The Rollerblade 7, Armageddon Boulevard,* etc.), as well as the big budget Hollywood films *Orgazmo* and *He Got Game.*

What kind of environment did you grow up in? Was it overly-strict, super liberal, or somewhere in the middle?

I lived with my mother half my childhood and with my father the other half. My father was very strict, but he was a cool kind of strict. You know, you've got to do your homework. Whether you had homework or not, you were in your room reading. School came easy for me; I was always a straight-A student. My mom was the complete opposite of my father. She probably overcompensated with me, because my father was so strict. It worked out pretty good for me because I got the balance of both book smarts and street smarts. We were not a real religious family, although both my mother and father had been raised Catholic. Their families had been pretty strict about it, but not my parents. They were pretty much like, "Do whatever you want." They didn't really push it.

You mentioned being a straight-A student in high school. I think there's a misconception that porn starlets are all going to be dumb airheads.

I guess it's like anything. There are the people who are smart with their money and treat it like a business, and now there are so many girls coming into the industry, because they want to be famous. Every girl is different, but there are very few who are able to take it a step beyond. I think either a girl's got it, or she doesn't. You could have the most beautiful girl and she not do as good as a girl who's completely average.

What are some of the differences between the girls who make it big and those who fade into instant obscurity?

Well, you know, there are girls we refer to as "A," "B," and "C" girls. The "A" girls are the prettier girls with the nice bodies. These are the contract girls who get the mass promotion. And then the "B" girls are the kind of cute girls, and the "C" girls are…well, they're the ones we don't use! [Laughs.] They're the ones who will do anything, and often they don't take very good care of themselves.

The prettier girls usually win, but not always. Sometimes the fans like the girls who are really nasty… The fans vary; they can like the prettiest girl and then they can like the girl who's the sluttiest. A lot of time it just has to do with timing and tastes, which are always different.

How old were you when you lost your virginity to a male and to a female respectively?

To a girl, I was ten. The girl was a friend. I came on to her while we were watching one of those *Emmanuelle* films. We played like we were sleeping, and we petted each other. I actually thought I was gay for a long time, because I liked girls so much. But now I realize I'm not gay. I like girls, but not like that… I like to have sex with girls, but that's about all they're good for—foreplay. Then I lost my virginity to a boy when I was thirteen, and I was with that same boy off and on until I was nineteen.

Before you began working in the adult film industry, you worked on "B" movies for the late Don Jackson. What was that like?

He shot a couple of "B" movies with Tiffany Million, who ultimately got me into adult films. Then he was shooting *Rollerblade 7* and Tiffany said, "Why don't you go meet with Don?" So I did, and they loved me, and I got along with Don excellently. He used me for a couple of different projects, and Tiffany moved on to porno. Then I kind of tagged along a year later after she asked me to be her date to an awards show.

How did your family react to the news that you were working in porn?

My mother knew before my husband killed himself. She had always wanted me to be a lawyer or a doctor—good things. "Smart girl" things. So she wanted me to do something else, but she knew that I was smart, and she just wanted me to be happy. My dad found out after my husband died, because half the girls who were at the funeral were wearing skimpy things, and because Ron Jeremy was there… There were girls there with boobs the size of my head. [Laughs.] At first my dad said something like, "Well, you've only done one of those movies, right?" Then someone at work told him they saw me on Howard Stern's show. Today my dad is okay with it. About three or four years ago, I got to take him to a convention and to the awards show. That way he could see what it was all about for himself, because people tend to get preconceived notions about these things.

It's like I always tell people, "Don't go on a porn shoot." The first time is exciting, but after a while everyone always says, "I can't look at porn the same way now." Because it's a business. Everyone has these preconceived notions. Even I did when Tiffany first told me she was doing porn, and I was pretty open-minded. I was like, "Oh, my God, you've got AIDS!" And this was like ten years ago. I was completely horrified, and I thought it was disgusting. I thought that everyone was always having sex that was unprotected and that they were all hookers. It's so funny.

What do you see as being some of the most common misconceptions the public tends to hold regarding the adult film industry?

That we're drug users and troubled teens who were molested. I think some people think we're forced to do this. Those seem to be the most common ones.

What was it like the first time you had sex in front of a camera and a room full of people?

The part that made me the most nervous was giving blowjobs. And this was with my first husband. I don't know—it just felt weird. It's not attractive, and it was just very awkward. But once you got into the sex part you, could hide; you didn't have to turn around. It's very scary at first, but then it becomes easier. At first, you see people come in, and they're nervous or excited. Then you see them a year later, and they're no longer fazed. They're just like, "Whatever."

Do you ever become so involved in what you're doing that you begin to forget those people are there?

Well, it depends on who you're working with. You're always aware that they're there, but to a lesser degree. It still feels good sometimes. It still can be a turn-on. That's just human nature, even if it is a business.

I would imagine that it would help to like sex. Could someone make it big in porn even if they didn't like sex?

Absolutely. I see it all the time. I think what happens is that you grow accustomed to it. Sex becomes just a normal routine part of the work environment. After a while, you lose the excitement and the butterflies, and you just become desensitized to it. That's what happened to me, so I decided it was time to get out. I got to the point where I didn't want to have sex anymore, and I even stopped masturbating. Now that I've stopped making films, I'm rediscovering my sexuality. It's like puberty all over again.

I mean, look, I worked almost every day for three or four years straight.

How many films on average does an "A" list performer appear in over the span of a year?

Myself, I never signed a contract. A contract girl could make ten. If she's hot, she'll work every day. Then it slows down, partially because your price then goes up. But in the beginning, even if she's not hot, everybody uses the girl because she's new. It's funny to hear the crew guys talk about the new girls. They're always like, "Man, she's hot." I always think, "let's see what they think next week." And by the next week, they don't think she's hot anymore. They don't even care anymore. Men are like lions; once they've had it or seen it, they don't care anymore.

I never wanted a contract. I wasn't interested in that. The contract helps you to make bigger money more quickly and become a bigger star, because you have a whole company behind you to promote you. My thing was to get into as many movies as I could because there are so many movies released. I'd appear in as many of them as I could. Fans are into certain types of movies, but I thought, if I'm in a whole bunch of them, I'll make more money.

Tell me about the fluffers.

That doesn't really happen. Basically the only time that happens is on gay shoots and on gangbang shoots. The reason they have them on those gangbang shoots is that this is usually when they have those really big gangbangs—like fifty guys—they'll sometimes have girls to get the guys prepared before they get to the main girl. Now this is all only what I've heard. I don't make films like that, but it's only when there are a whole bunch of guys, like fifty or one hundred. Those are the only times that's done. I think that's just another old myth about the porn industry. Then people hear about those gangbang films, and they hear about the fluffers, and they say, "See, it does exist!"

So if a girl started out as a fluffer, would that pretty much be a career-ender, or could they actually build a career on that?

Usually that's a girl that you wouldn't want to be seen anywhere with. [Laughs.] That's one of those girls that you definitely ride on your moped with a helmet on. I'm sorry, but I'm just being honest.

Who have been your favorite onscreen sexual partners?

Janine is my favorite girl. There's just an aura she has about her. She's very sexy. Very hot. She's always been my favorite girl. And I guess my favorite guy would be my second husband, Julian, again because he was so hot. I mean, why wouldn't I want to be with the hot ones? [Laughs.] Other than that, it would probably be Tom Byron. I haven't worked with him in years, but I worked with him a lot when I first got started. Tom was *nasty.* [Laughs again.]

Do you have many people approach you on the street and say, "Hey, you're Jill Kelly"?

Yes. Even when I wear sunglasses and a hat. I don't look like those other girls. I have a very distinctive look; long face, long nose, high cheek bones. It's pretty hard for me to hide. I've been out with no makeup on, wearing a big hat and sunglasses, and people still seem to recognize me wherever I go. I think it's because I have a very unique look, and because I've done so many films.

Do you get approached by many mainstream celebrities?

Yeah. That's probably the coolest thing about all of this.

Like who?

I'd better not say. I don't really feel that's fair to them.

Have you had many incidents with scary or obsessive fans?

I've only had one scary fan. That was back when I'd only been in the business for about two years. The Internet was just starting to get big at that time, and there was a website that showed how to find your favorite porn star. And, of course, they used me as the example! My mother was actually staying with me at the time. I was living about two hours from Los Angeles, so I was always getting home very late. So this guy kept coming to my house, and he would be sitting outside. And I had really mean dogs. Well, one time when my mother and I were there, he was out in the backyard, and the dogs were completely fine with him! I called the cops, and I got nowhere. It took them over an hour to get there, and he was gone by then.

Two or three days later, my mother was there all by herself. She was doing the laundry, and she came into my bedroom… All my movies were gone. He also took a pair of boots and my dildos. There was money and jewelry there, but he didn't touch that stuff. And usually, that's either going to cause somebody to escalate this behavior or relieve it. Luckily, that was the last we ever saw of him.

Other than that, I received one death threat a couple of years ago. It was right before CES, so that was scary. Most of the time I just get letters from religious people. "I'm going to save you and help you to get Jesus into your heart." Whatever. Then they say something like, "By the way, in such and such movie, you looked really great!" [Laughs.] It's like, what are you talking about?

Have you ever had sex with a fan?

Yes. I have a thing for guys giving each other head. At that time, I had a boyfriend who will remain nameless. This was in Sacramento, and there was this kid who wanted to come home with me. So I told him I'd take him home, but he had to do whatever I told him to do. [Laughs.] It was actually a lot of fun, and he seemed to enjoy himself quite a bit.

There have been a couple of other fans. It's just a case of the right place, right time. I don't just sleep around. You know, it's once in a blue moon, when circumstances happen to be just right… I've been in a lot of relationships because I don't like to date. I hate dating. It's not comfortable. You don't really know that person, and they're not who they're going to be in six months after they've become comfortable around you. Everybody's on their best behavior in the beginning. Then, down the road, you're like, who is this person?

This is kind of a two-part question. How difficult is it to maintain a relationship with someone outside the adult film industry, and is it any easier to maintain a relationship with someone else in the business?

It's absolutely impossible either way. Usually, the guy starts out liking the girl *because* she's in porn. It's a turn-on to him. Then the jealousy starts to set in. He can't help it. I even meet people who are swingers—where both people are having sex with other people—and they still get jealous. And remember, the business is so open that the girls or the guys will just come up to each other in front of their partners and start talking about those things. If they weren't in the business, and they came up and started talking about those things, the guy or girl would knock them out. So it can be a lot for someone who's not in the business to deal with.

It's not any easier when you're dating someone in the business. Maybe the guy doesn't like another guy the girl has to have sex with, or maybe he's jealous because the other guy has a bigger dick... I'm serious. These are things that routinely happen. The guys will say, "I don't want you working with that guy" because maybe he's a little bit rough or simply because he's got a bigger dick. And then maybe the girl doesn't want him to work with another girl, because she doesn't like her or she thinks she's a slut or whatever.

I've never seen a relationship work in the business. Never, ever, ever. Even Nina Hartley. I mean, she was the one person who I thought had it made. She had a husband and a wife. And now none of them are together, and they were all together for a long, long time.

Everyone assumes the sex life of a porn star must be pretty wild. At its wildest, how wild was your sex life?

You know, a couple of orgies here and there, and those were with pretty much the same people. That's about it. I mean, I did so much stuff on camera that I didn't need that in my personal life. Probably the wildest thing I've done was the bi-sexual guy thing. Nothing too far-out there. I don't know. I mean, I've had sex with a lot of women. I had a lot of three-ways. I suppose those things are out of the norm for the average person.

HYAPATIA LEE

PORN LEGEND HYAPATIA LEE was born Vickie Lynch in Indianapolis, Indiana, in 1960 to a fifteen-year-old mother. Because of this,
she was raised by her grandmother, a full-blooded Cherokee, who raised
her with a healthy respect for her Indian heritage. As a teen, she attended
Butler University, where she studied theatre and dance. She soon began
performing in local plays and dinner theaters. She entered and won top
honors in the Miss Nude Galaxy contest in 1979 and 1981, becoming the
first and only two-time winner. She then became an erotic dancer, which
ultimately led to her entrance into the adult film industry in 1983. Because
she had won the Miss Nude Galaxy contest twice, Lee had a following before she ever filmed her first scene. The first adult film performer to be
given an exclusive contract (with Caribbean Films), and also the first Native American porn actress, Lee made her adult film debut in *The Young
Like It Hot*. (Although she technically made *Naughty Girls Need Love Too*
first, the film was not released until after *The Young Like It Hot*.)

Lee quickly established herself as one of the biggest stars of the so-
called "Golden Age of Porn." A favorite among viewers, Lee won numerous awards, including Best Actress and Female Fan Favorite. She wrote
and directed a number of her own films and strove for a level of excellence
in her films in an industry in which the quality of the product was on the
decline. "During the Golden Age, we made real movies that just happened
to have sex in them," Lee has said. One such film was 1985's *Ribald Tales
of the Canterbury*, which Lee herself adapted from Geoffrey Chaucer. Shot
for a then-astounding $300,000—making it the most expensive X-rated
film (other than *Caligula*) ever made—the film was ultimately named the
finest adult feature ever produced.

In 1990, Lee was elected president of the X-Rated Actors Association,
which was an organization formed to protect performers' rights to onscreen condom use. Lee retired in 1993, having made approximately thirty-

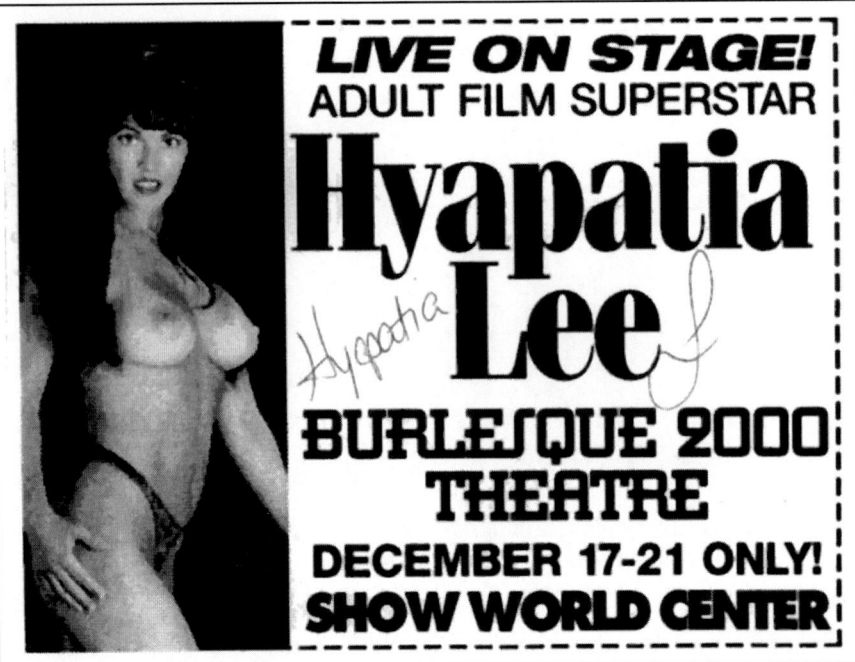

Actress Hyapatia Lee is considered one of the finest performers from the 'Golden Age' of adult film. She retired in 1993 having made only 36 films.

six films. (It should be noted that scenes from her films have since been reedited into approximately sixty compilation films.) She has since been inducted into both the XRCO and AVN Hall of Fame and has been named one of the twenty-five greatest performers ever to work in the business.

KEY PORN TITLES: *Ribald Tales of the Canterbury, Naughty Girls Need Love Too,* and *Indian Summer.*

MAINSTREAM CRED: Hyapatia Lee has appeared in the feature films *Killing Obsession* and *The Wacky Adventures of Doctor Boris and Nurse Shirley,* as well as the documentary *What Do You Say to a Naked Lady?*.

What was your childhood like?

I grew up with grandmother. Neither my mother nor my father were in the picture since they were very young when they had me. My grandmother was a wonderful Native American woman, who raised me with a lot of the traditions intact. I learned to speak Cherokee. We were very close.

Would you say it was a liberal upbringing?

It certainly wasn't a traditional religious upbringing. I know a lot of people are raised to go to church every Sunday and stuff like that... It wasn't like that because we were not necessarily Christians. We were Native American traditionalists. So I was always taught about the Great Spirit, but not that there was any certain day set aside to worship the Great Spirit. That was something you were supposed to do all the time. And not in a special place. If there was a special place to worship the Great Spirit, it was outside, because that was what the Great Spirit made. You know, it would be kind of stupid to chop down a tree and build a church and show God how I can do it better! [Laughs.]

How did you get into the adult film industry?

I first started in theater. Then I started doing dinner theater. And then several events in my life sort of took me off track... A good friend of mine was a dancer in a club downtown, and I started dancing basically because she was an influence in my life, and I knew how much money she was making. And I loved to dance. I was basically a dance major at Butler University, but there's not a lot of call for dancers in Indianapolis that make a lot of money in any other way. And that club had a lot of featured dancers that came in from the road, and every week there'd be a different feature. Those features would tell me about agents that booked them on the road. Then I won the Miss Nude Galaxy award and went out on the road, dancing as a feature stripper. Then I got on the circuit, and the same people who owned Caribbean Films owned all these theaters. And I had heard of one of the other actresses—I won't say who—snorting cocaine off the candy counter in the lobby and dancing barefoot with the same dirty negligee every show. And she was making something like $6,000 a week! And I thought, Wait a minute, I do much better shows than that... I do a fire show where I set myself on fire, I do a robot show where I'm carried on the stage, I do belly dancer shows... So I wondered why I wasn't making as much money as she was. Well, it was all because of the movies.

So I decided to get into the movies that way. I contacted the people who had booked me into those theaters since they owned Caribbean Films, and that's kind of how it all came to be.

Where did your stage name Hyapatia come from?

It's a Cherokee name. I believe it's somewhat of a takeoff from Hypatia, the Greek philosopher and mathematician. I liked the name. There was a cousin of mine who had died at childbirth who had that name, and I thought it was a beautiful name.

Tell me about the first adult feature you made.

The first one I actually made was called *Naughty Girls Need Love Too*, which was for Essex Films. Caribbean Films had flown me out to California and got me prepared to do the two movies I was supposed to do for them, one of which I wrote, and it turned out that the people they wanted to shoot with weren't ready. So I was stuck out in California without much to do, and not making much money… [Laughs.] So they made a deal with Essex Films that I would do that movie, but they had to release it after the Caribbean movie came out.

What was it like the first time you were in front of the camera? Were you nervous?

Not really. It was kind of like being on stage only with not as many people. It was such an intimate environment… I was kind of used to being in front of people and performing. I mean, the first time I was ever on stage and did a solo dance was when I was four years old. So I had kind of been dancing and performing all my life. So then the things I did in Indianapolis were musical comedies, which required singing and acting. So this was kind of old hat for me. And as far as the sexual part, I just looked at it as a part I had to play. So how would this girl, who's had this and this happen in her past, have sex?

Would you say that you were a sexual person prior to your working in the business?

Yes. Very.

What was your family's reaction to the news that you were working in the adult film industry?

Well, my grandmother wasn't very happy. My aunt and uncle weren't very happy either. They'd known I'd been dancing, and they weren't very happy about that. But they got used to the idea. They didn't approve, but they still loved me.

I've read that today you regret having worked in the adult film industry?

Not really. I have regrets in regards to how the business was done and how it could have been so much better, but I don't regret doing the work. These films are sold by whose name is on the cover and who's in it—not by the director or the action the way mainstream movies might be. They're sold basically by the actress on the cover and the actress in the film. So when you go to a regular mainstream movie, the person whose name is selling the film, be it the actor, the director, or the producer, gets a lot of money. They get residuals. They continue to get paid every time the product is sold or viewed. In this business, it does not work that way. You get a couple hundred, maybe a couple thousand dollars, and that's the end of it. And that's just not fair. I mean, it's the girl that's selling the film. They're not buying it because it's a Caribbean Film or an Essex Film, or because Eddie Summers directed it. They could give a shit less about that. [Laughs.] They're looking at the girl on the cover or looking for a name that's their favorite girl. And that's who should be getting the money.

You're in more compilations than you are in features. What are your thoughts on that?

Oh yeah, because I really didn't do that many films. It's a drag. In regular movies, you can't just cut out an action scene and stick it in a compilation of action scenes and sell that. And the worst part of it is that none of the performers get any money from that. None of those girls who were involved with any of those compilation films ever got a cent from any of them. And it's wrong.

You were married to producer/director/actor Bud Lee. Was it easier or more difficult being married to someone else who was working in the industry?

We both got into the business at the same time. I was the first one who did anything in the business. I didn't really want to work with a lot of different people, so part of the deal was that I would work with my husband. So that's how he got into the business.

Did working with exclusively with Bud hurt the amount of work that you got?

No. I was already limited in the amount of work I was going to do anyway. I was under contract to only do two films per year. That lasted three years. So there was no way I was going to make any more than six films anyway. So it didn't matter. Besides, I didn't want to make a whole slew of films. I wanted to be very selective. I wanted to do movies that I had written or movies that I had sung the theme song to, like in *Body Girls*, or movies that I thought had good roles. I was in it for the acting. I never did any of that crap where it was "knock, knock, who's there? The pizza delivery guy." I wanted character development. I wanted the character to change during the course of the film. I wanted character arc. I want something that I can sink my teeth into as an actress.

When you entered the business, there was a lot more acting required than there is today.

And that was the aspect of the films that I enjoyed the most. That and dancing. In *Body Girls*, I did a ballet sequence that I choreographed. Paul Thomas wrote a song for the film, and he played the piano and sang the song while I danced. That was a dream segment. That kind of stuff was a lot of fun. That's why I was there.

Do you think that most porn performers are really frustrated legitimate actors?

When I was in the business, yes, absolutely. But when I was getting out of the business, there were girls who were just in it for the sex. They just wanted to have sex with anything that walked, so they figured they might as well get paid for it. Those girls would do any kind of scene— anals, three-ways… All the kinds of stuff that I wouldn't do. That was a different kind of person than people like myself or Porsche Lynn or Megan Leigh or Colleen Brennan. We were actresses. Porn had already kind of changed, but when I got into the business in the Eighties, there were still more actresses than people who just enjoyed the sex. That's why we were there.

The product of the adult film industry changed a lot between your debut in 1983 and your swan song in 1993.

The production value was ridiculously low when I quit. When I first started the average movie was between $80,000 and $120,000 to make. They were shot on film—35mm Panavision. I made a film called *The Ribald Tales of Canterbury*, which I wrote and adapted from Chaucer's *Canterbury Tales*. That was a $300,000 budget movie. Other than *Caligula*, that was the most expensive X-rated movie ever made. That's what I was into. Then along came video. I took a year off and had a baby. When I came back, I found that everything had changed. "We're all shooting on video, and because we're shooting on video, and we're saving money on our medium that we're shooting on, we're gonna go ahead and go haywire and say we'll pay you half." I would say that I was doing the same amount of work, but they would say, "Yeah, but it's for video." I don't care! I don't care if you're shooting it in black-and-white, it's still the same act. You know, I'm still doing the same thing. Why am I not getting paid the same?

Did it seem like there was less attention to detail at that time?

Yeah. Before, we were making movies for $80,000 and $120,000. And when you got down to the $80,000 films they would call it a "three day wonder." You know, they were gonna put it together in three days, and you were gonna wonder how they did it so quickly. Nowadays, they shoot movies in less than one day. And it's easy to see why and how—they don't have any freaking dialogue! [Laughs.] That was very frustrating to me. Like I said before, I was really into it for the acting and the production value. I thought we were bridging the gap between an R-rated movie and something where you just threw the sheets back when the action got hot. Yes, it was still X-rated, but it was an entertaining film to watch just for its own value and story. It was like an R-rated movie that just took it a little further, instead of something that's nothing but sex from the beginning to the end with no reason why.

You mentioned working on The Ribald Tales of the Canterbury. *What was that experience like?*

It was wonderful. We shot for nine days. We used the costumes from Universal Studios. These were the original costumes that were used in *Camelot*. There was horseback stuff… Riding, I mean. Nothing kinky. [Laughs.] Everything was authentic. I had to write it like, "What wilt thou say?" It was really neat. I loved it. We had people hired for that film who were just actors. They had no sex. Their job was just to act. They loved it too, because they believed in what we were doing. We had a miller's wheel inside a studio. We had a roasted pig with an apple in the mouth and everything. Even the tables were authentic. It was just fabulous. It was so much fun, and everyone enjoyed working on that. When it was all over, we were all so sad to see everybody go.

Did you write and direct as a means to gain some control over your image and the types of films you were in?

It actually started out of frustration. When I first came to Caribbean Films and signed my contract, they said, "Here's the first movie you're doing." And they gave me this thirteen page handwritten script. I looked at that and said, "You have got to be kidding." And they were like, "No. Why? Do you think you can make it better?" And I said, "Uh, let me just try, okay?" [Laughs.] So I took it home and started writing. I had studied theatre. I figured plays were no different from movies—you just put 'em in front of a camera. Then it's the cameraman's job to figure out where to shoot it from and all that. So it was really easy. I put characters in there who were really believable, who said things that real people would really say. It still led up to sex, but it did it in a more natural realistic way.

You were the only Native American performer working in the adult film industry, and the producers certainly played up that fact. Did you ever feel that they were exploiting or disrespecting your heritage?

At the end, I really did. They had me doing lines like, "I can't have another drink. I'm Native American, and you know what'll happen." Or there was "Don't get her mad, she'll scalp you." [Laughs.] I was thinking, this is just a little racist here. Again, that really didn't happen until the end. It was frustrating. That was mostly Vivid Video's doing.

And your Penthouse *layout was titled "Indian Giver."*

Yeah, I thought that was kind of weird, too.

You were working in the industry in the early Eighties when AIDS first reared its ugly head. That must have been a frightening time to work in adult film.

The more and more that AIDS was talked about, and the more prevalent it became, the more I decided I wanted to work with a condom. So, many of my scenes are with condoms, and those are the later ones I shot. At first, Vivid Video, whom I was under contract with at the time, didn't have any problem with that. And other girls decided they wanted to work with condoms, as well, and Vivid didn't have any problems with that. Then all of a sudden someone said the horrible "U" word, which was union. And I got elected to be a union leader for the women.

Was this the X-Rated Actors Association?

Yes. We all got together and tried to make rules that would be good for everybody. I mean, I had been lying in bed when lights were exploding over me, and if I hadn't moved in time I'd have been badly burned. There were a lot of unsafe set practices at the time. There were fires on sets so many times I can't count them. I mean, we had crews working twenty-four hours a day. It's not good when your gaffer is working that many hours, and he's a little tired, and he might not remember exactly how much electricity he's got going to this, that, or whatever. We kind of wanted to make it a little safer, a little more respectable—not only safe sex, but safe in every way.

And that started such a big hullabaloo, and all the businesses got so angry about the whole thing. They had a meeting and invited all the talent, and they said they wouldn't hire anyone who would only work with a condom. And of course we had to say, "We need to take a stand here where people refuse to work without a condom." I mean, they were using condoms in all the scenes in gay porno movies, and those were selling. Why couldn't we? This made no sense to me. Safe sex was safe sex. You know, I've even had people come up to me and say, "Your movies are great and all, but when you start to have sex, and there's no condom, I start to worry, and I can't enjoy the film." And of course, the companies didn't want to give in.

And then we had the head of the National World Health Association's task force on AIDS come in and talk to us. He had all of us sitting in a studio in Van Nuys. Everybody was there—all the directors, producers, and talent. And he told us basically that we were like a tribe because we had sex amongst ourselves so frequently. He said that if one person in this so-called tribe would contract AIDS, then it would pass like wildfire. That made a lot of sense to people like myself and other actresses who were just in the business to act and have fun while they were acting. Other actresses got up on stage and said, "Well, I've decided that if I'm having sex with a condom, then it's not real sex." The guy was really disheartened by this response; most of the people were against the condoms, and were verbal about this. He said, "You know, there are twelve-year-old prostitutes in Thailand that are smarter than you guys." So he left in disgust, and about twelve of us chased him out to his car and said, "I want you to know that you have not wasted your time. We really appreciated your talk. We listened, and we learned a lot from it. We're not going to work without condoms anymore, or we're just not going to work." He was happy to hear that. And, as far as I know, all of the people who made that commitment stuck to it. I think most of us just quit because we were so disgusted by all of it.

First of all, they didn't want to pay us what we were worth when people were buying the movies based on who was in them. Why shouldn't the actress who's the reason they're buying the movie in the first place make the lion's share of the money? And I don't mean, "Let's give her $1,000 instead of $950." I'm talking about getting paid based on how much the film makes. I'm talking about residuals; maybe five cents a box, you know? But no, they wouldn't budge. Then there was this, the condom issue. They didn't care about our lives. There were people in this meeting with the producers who said, "It doesn't matter if you guys die from AIDS anyway, because none of you have any family." So your life doesn't matter if you don't have a family, I guess. And I'm sitting there saying, "I have children." And I wasn't the only one there who had children—almost everyone there had kids. Then Randy West stands up and says, "If you're so worried about your life, then why don't you wear your seatbelt?" I said, "I wear a seatbelt every time I get in the car, before the car is even started. Why don't you wear a condom?" And it came down to the fact that he was older, and he had never performed with a condom. If it's going to take a few more minutes, then big deal.

Was that the primary reason for your retirement?

Yes.

You were a contract girl throughout your career. Are there any disadvantages to being under contract as opposed to being a free agent?

I found the disadvantage to be that you weren't working as much as the other girls, which can lead some people to believe that because of that, you aren't as popular. I guess a lot of the guys don't realize that you can be offered a job and decide not to do it. Just because you're not making twenty movies every six months doesn't mean that you're not being offered that.

I kind of modeled my career after Marilyn Chambers. She only made like nine X-rated movies, yet she's extremely popular. It's because the movies she chose to make were so good. And that's what I was trying to do. So in regards to that, being under contract was a definite advantage, because I could wait and do two good movies a year. That was what we did, and I think it worked out well in terms of popularity. I was able to do all kinds of magazine layouts—I think I was in just about every men's magazine that was out there at least once.

Do you ever miss the attention you received as an adult film star?

Yeah, I do. [Laughs.] I have to be honest. For many years I didn't. I was really happy just being secluded out in the country in southern Indiana, just hiding on my acreage. I live in the woods, and nobody can see my house from the road. I'm all hidden, and that was great. That was cool for about ten years. And then I thought, "well, it was kind of nice when everybody was applauding."

EVELYN LIN

EVELYN LIN was born in Hunan, China, in 1987. Her family relocated to Southern California in 1991 when she was four years old. Intent on becoming an import model, she was "tricked by some jackass photographer" into shooting her first adult film and inking her first contract with Home Grown Video in 2005 at the age of 18. However, she never looked back, as she quickly discovered that being on camera felt natural to her and that she enjoyed the work. "Under the hot lights," she has said, "my bad girl side really came out. As someone once described me, I was like a wildcat for the camera."

Lin is currently attending college at the University of California, San Diego (UCSD) as a Communications major by day and working as an adult film starlet by night. When she's not at school or filming, she enjoys hanging out with her friends and partying. She also enjoys skiing at Mammoth Mountain, biking, "attempting to surf," running her own website, and watching detective shows like *CSI: Las Vegas* and *NCIS*. She has also auctioned off a dinner date with herself on eBay to raise money for the American Society for the Prevention of Animals. (The date went for just under $1,000.)

"I think the crazy thing about me is that I'm caught between two stereotypes: sappy romantic and crazy nymphomaniac," she says. "I love to be treated like a princess and just cuddled during romantic movies. On the other hand, I am seriously addicted to sex. Most of my ex-boyfriends couldn't keep up with how much I wanted. I never thought I'd hear a guy beg me for less sex!"

Lin has appeared in more than 100 adult films to date. She has also made appearances in the adult magazines *Barely Legal*, *Tight*, and *Oriental Women*.

KEY PORN TITLES: *Smokin' Hot Asians, Young Asian Cuties 4,* and *Cockasian 2006.*

In a few short years, actress Evelyn Lin has established herself as one of the biggest stars in adult cinema.

What was your childhood like?

You know, I just had a normal childhood. I would say I grew up in a mostly Asian community. So I've been around a lot of Asian traditions. I would consider it a pretty normal childhood. I didn't have anything traumatic happen. A lot of people always assume that because I do porn, that I was messed up somehow in my childhood, but I had a perfectly normal childhood.

What were you like as a child?

I would say I was very shy to strangers. I've always been really shy meeting new people. I mean, I always loved the camera. I have some friends who are like, "Oh, my gosh, I could never have done this as a kid, because I was terrified of the camera." I was okay with the camera, but shy meeting new people.

What sort of student were you?

I would say I was a pretty good student. I was always getting pretty good grades. Honor roll, and stuff like that. I don't know if you've heard of a program called G.A.T.E.? It's an acronym for Gifted and Talented in Education, I think. It's a special program for kids who are like the honor roll students, and I was in that. So I would say I was a pretty good student.

Are you, or were you at any time, what you would call religious?

I would say that I don't go to church or believe in a structured religion, but I do agree with a lot of the ideals that religions teach. You know, like don't cheat, don't steal, don't kill somebody… I just see them as guidelines for a good, moral person. So I wouldn't say I'm religious, but I believe in a lot of the teachings. I do believe that there could be a higher power—there's just no telling.

Did you attend church as a child?

I went to church a couple of times and didn't really find it was for me. I didn't really feel it was teaching what I thought religion should be, but, you know, it was too structured for me. It was very, "Follow these guidelines, or you're going to go to hell." That didn't seem very open, loving—what I thought religion should be.

How old were you when you had your first sexual experience?

We just messed around. I think I was 16. Late bloomer. I actually never had a boyfriend until I was 15.

How old were you when you lost your virginity?

I was seventeen.

Did you find that experience to be a comfortable one?

First time having sex? No. Definitely not. I'm sure other women out there can relate to this, but it hurt like hell. I'm actually kind of surprised, thinking back on it. I just remember thinking, "God, this friggin' hurts." I don't know why I continued to do it, but I guess after the first time, it was like, "Oh, I guess this is as awesome as everyone claims it is." [Laughs.]

When did you decide to get into the adult film industry, and had you been thinking about this for a while?

It was 2005, so I was 18. This photographer—I feel really foolish thinking back on it now—but, basically, I was working with a photographer that I trusted, and he said that if I wanted to do import modeling, which is originally what I wanted to do, that if I shot one or two scenes in the porn industry, that would get me recognition, and that would make it easier to get into import modeling. I guess now, thinking back on it, there were some holes in his story, but I kind of wanted to try it anyway. I did actually think about it for quite a few months, because he propositioned me for this maybe a couple of months after I turned 18. I didn't shoot until April, and my birthday had been in August. So I was getting closer to 19—halfway there, I guess. I really thought about it a long time. Do I want to do this? And, obviously, I chose to do it.

Did you first discuss this with people you were close to?

I discussed it with my best friend. I discussed it with a bunch of my close friends, and they were like, "It's really up to you, because it's your life. We understand that this is your decision. We understand that you're still the same person. This doesn't change anything about your personality. You're still my friend, and it's really up to you." They really gave me support and let me know that there would be someone there for me. I didn't have to go into it alone, I guess.

I've had adult performers tell me that they've lost work in other fields after someone discovered that they were working in porn. Do you see that as an issue?

That's definitely an issue. I'm not going to shoot porn forever and ever. I'm not looking to do GILF porn, so I'm eventually going to have to get a real job. I don't want it to be out *everywhere* that this is what I do. Personally, I think that this would have nothing to do with my job performance, but some companies and some people care.

What was your first porn set experience like?

Well, it was raining in Los Angeles, which it rarely does. And it was in April or May, and I was late by two hours maybe. I just wasn't used to making the drive into the valley at that time, because I wasn't living in the valley. I thought, "Oh, I'll just drive into L.A. It'll take an hour tops." First off, it was raining, and then there was traffic. I was totally late. So I was more concerned about being late, so that "Oh, my gosh, I'm late, I'm late!" is all that was going through my mind. It kind of pushed that I was about to shoot a porno for the first time completely out of my head. When I got there, with my being late and all, they were like, "Okay, let's get you to sign a release, and let's get you shooting." So it just kind of happened in a blur. Before I knew it, I was naked and taking pictures, and by that time, I guess it was kind of…the shock hadn't set in yet, so I didn't really think about it, but, you know, I just shot the scene, and I was like, "Okay, that actually kind of felt normal." I know a lot of people say, "Aren't you really nervous?" I was surprised I didn't get nervous, because I'm someone who has been known to get stage fright. Everyone who was on set was like, "Oh, a new girl, let's watch." There were actually a lot of people crowded in the room, just watching me, I guess. I don't know. It all went so normally for me, I didn't really think about it as being weird or something I should be nervous about. It was just shooting porn. It felt normal, I guess.

You are currently going to college, correct?

Yeah.

Do you make adult films to pay for college?

I have loans and stuff like that, but it definitely makes it easier, because I have a lot of friends that have a really, really hard time paying for college. They have their loans and stuff like that, but books can cost $600 for one quarter. You're just like, "Oh, my gosh!" If you just had a normal working job, *and* you are trying to go to college, it's really, really stressful, because then you have absolutely *no* time to study. You are so tired from your job that you go home and fall asleep. I have had friends like that, and it really affects their grades. I'd say my first year of porn, it was definitely hard balancing shooting, but I kind of got used to how much time it takes. It's definitely easier than going to a full-time job, and then having to go to college.

Would you say you started in adult because of interest in sex, or money, or a combination of the two, or something else?

Like I said before, I just wanted to do modeling in general. It was a combination of always having loved sex, and the amounts of money they were saying for just having sex. I was like, "Oh, holy cow!" You know? I guess it was combination of wanting to do modeling, and money, and sex.

How long do you envision your adult career lasting?

That's a hard one, because when I first started I was thinking it was going to be maybe a week. At the end of the week, I was like, "Oh, okay, I'm getting ready to quit." You know, it wasn't a hard job. My agent called me back, and she was like, "Hey, you want to shoot another scene?" I was like, "You know what? Sure, I'm just going to do like a weekend-only thing." I'm not shooting as much as I was before. That was really hard to keep up with. Especially this one where we shot everyday or every other day, and I was just so tired. Since I'm not shooting so much now, it doesn't take up as much time, so I can't really say when it'll end. My rule before was that it was really taking up a lot of my time, and I wouldn't be able to hold down a regular job or anything, but since I'm shooting for my own website right now, it's hard to say. I shoot when I have time.

Would you say you make more off the videos or the website?

If I was shooting videos more consistently... If I was shooting like once a day, I would definitely say shooting for these big companies. My website is like $20 a membership. It's actually only me and my webmaster running the site. It's not like some big company running it and promoting it. I don't do advertisements. It's a small-run website. It's how you would compare a multi-million corporation versus a small mom and pop shop. I would definitely say shooting for the big companies is more lucrative.

Do you consider yourself an exhibitionist?

Yes. I would definitely say that. I mean, even outside of porn, I guess. I don't mind going to the nude beach, stripping down, and getting naked. Even though I'm like the only female there. Or I've had sex in a car or in an elevator and stuff like that. It's a different kind of thrill, the risk of being caught. I've never done it too crazy, but just a little bit.

Did you have any interest in pornography prior to your entering the adult film industry?

Yes. Definitely. It kind of weirded out my guy friends once in a while, because I'm like, "Hey, do you have any good porn? Can I borrow it?" And they were always like, "What the heck? No, you can't borrow my porn." I'm like, "Oh, come on. I'm sure you've lent your guy buddies your porn." "No, that's weird. Why do you want to watch porn?" And I'm like, "What does it matter? It's sexy." I've had fans who are couples message me, and they're like, "Oh, you know, we have sex while we watch your movies." And I'm like, "Hey, I used to do that, too!"

Do you think your liking porn led to your interest in doing porn?

Yeah, I would definitely say so. I thought it was going to be more along the lines of how feature films are shot. My favorite before I got into porn was *Debbie Does Dallas 2*, with Sunrise Adams. I was interested in there being a story. I'm interested in getting into that. I haven't shot one yet, but I'll keep my fingers crossed.

What does it take to be a successful porn actress?

I definitely think that a lot of the fans want you to go more and more hardcore, which is a little hard for me, because the first four scenes I shot were anal, penetration, anal, and anal. So that was really rough for my first week. I was like, I can't do this every day. I think I'll die from exhaustion! [Laughs.] So I dropped down to just boy-girl, and I feel like a lot of my fans are like, "Why won't you shoot anal anymore?" I do for my own website, because I can take my time. I can take it as slow as I want. Or as gentle as I want, but on a real set and for a big company, they won't be, "Oh, okay, take your time. We'll go gentle." So a lot of fans are like, "Why don't you do anal anymore?" It's hard for me to go up, you know? Like a lot of people start out doing just girl-girl, and then they do boy-girl, so that explodes like a whole new area. It's like a whole new kind of scene that the companies can shoot, and the girls keep getting hired.

I would definitely say that to make it really big, you have to have bigger boobs. Or get implants. I've entertained the idea at one point or another, but I've had so many fans tell me not to.

Do you have rules for your male costars?

I do. Please don't spit on me. I know sometimes things get a little rough. You can pull my hair, you can spank my ass, but I'm not really into the spitting or the choking. And definitely, if I squirm, because you're playing with my clit too much, it's because it's really sensitive so please go easy on that. That's about it. I would say I'm a pretty easy person to work with. I don't have too many restrictions or rules. No spitting or choking, don't try to stick your finger in my butt if it's a regular scene, and not an anal scene. Don't be too crazy with the clit play, because I'm really sensitive.

How frequently are your on-camera orgasms real, and how often are they fake?

I would say it's probably 70/30, like seventy-percent real and thirty-percent fake. A lot of the scenes, they're like, "We want you to come multiple times!" And I'm like, "Uh, I haven't learned that talent yet. I wish I could."

Would you say the majority of times when you're faking it is when they're asking for multiple orgasms?

Multiple ones, or it's just some crazy position. You're like "You know, this looks really good on camera, but I prefer a different thing to actually come."

Do you consider yourself a sexual person off-screen?

Yes. I would definitely consider myself a sexual person off-screen. I've had boyfriends from the past that when we're having sex, they're like, "You know, can we not have sex as much as we do? I'm really tired. Five times a day is a little much for us." I've always been into trying new things. I own handcuffs, just for personal usage, and I played with bondage gear. Nothing too hardcore—just cuffs , bedstraps, and over-the-door handcuffs. I actually bought bondage tape. That was interesting. I played with wax and different toys. I think my toy collection is a little scary. I have a huge bag in my closet. I'm always afraid someone's going to be like, "Oh,

I need something out of your closet," and my toy collection is going to come spilling out on them! [Laughs.]

I would definitely say I'm a very sexual person, but I've actually gotten safer since I've gotten in the industry, just because I know so much about STDs. Since I'm getting tested monthly, I feel better about having a little bit more fun; not having to worry as much, and I require long-term partners to do the same thing.

The majority of your films are Asian-themed. Does this ever make you want to do something different?

I don't really mind it. Some of the things, you know, are a little kooky and a little out there. I remember one I shot where they had the guy with a bowl of rice and chopsticks—clinking on a bowl with chopsticks—"*Come hereeee!*" Then I follow the sound of the chopsticks and rice bowl to him. A lot of people get offended by all these Asian stereotypes that they portray, but the people I work with on set don't really believe all of this stuff. They just think it's as funny as I do. They understand that some people want to see really, really stereotyped [characters]. So I just think it's really fun, you know? I mean, I'm Asian, so I don't really mind it.

I wouldn't mind doing a feature that's not so Asian-oriented, but I don't mind it. It's more the whole young girl thing. I've actually shot a lot of young girl scenes. I couldn't wait to get out of that, because the pigtails were a little too much sometimes. I wanted to do sexy and not so bubbly. Normally I'm a bubbly person, but it was over the top and a little me feeling like jailbait.

Have you ever been concerned with the content of anything you've been offered or filmed?

If I didn't ever really like something, I turned it down. For example, there's a website that does pretty hardcore bondage stuff with hogties, and water suspension, and water pussy, and stuff like that. They were like, "We want you to shoot with us." And I was just like, "Yeah, no. That's a little too scary for me."

Now that you mention it, yes. They made me fuck a Yeti in *Babysitting #25* by Notorious. That thing often gives me nightmares. They had the guy wear a gorilla costume or something. They made him put on a scary mask. First off, that mask gave me nightmares for weeks! Seriously. The first time I saw it, I screamed for real. That one gets around a lot to my friends, and they're kind of like, "I can't believe you fucked a Yeti." I'm like, "I can't believe I fucked a Yeti, either." That one I definitely kind of wish I hadn't shot. I mean, I guess it gets people talking about me, but not necessarily in a good way.

Are there any sex acts that you refuse to do?

Double-stuffing. First off, I'm not into that. But also, I think it's physically impossible. So definitely no double-stuffing.

Do you enjoy watching yourself having sex in your films?

I guess it depends on the film. Some of the films, like the young girl ones, where they're like, "Act really, really innocent and naïve." I'm like, "No, that's not really me, not my personality." For the most part, yeah, I enjoy watching it. Normally when you have sex, you don't have all those crazy lights on. You don't have all that crazy make up on, and the hair done, and all that stuff. I'm like, "Hey, that's kind of sexy."

Who are some of your favorite actors to work with, and why?

For females, and she's actually left the business now, but Lana Croft. We just get along really well and have great chemistry on set. She's a really good friend. I've actually become really good friends with her off-set. She understands that this feels better or this looks better. So we have a very good communication on set. For guys, I'd say James Dean. It drives producers crazy when I say that, because they're like, "He's so expensive!" Yeah, I shot with him, and we had a really good chemistry, and I was like, "Wow, this guy…" Definitely James, maybe because he's closer to my age, and I think it helps us connect a little more. Usually the guys I shoot with are a lot older.

What's the oddest on-set experience you've had?

That would definitely be that Yeti scene, I think. The whole premise of the story was that I'm telling scary bedtime stories, and I guess I fall asleep. Then I have a nightmare, and this monster that looks like Yeti is coming, and I say, "Oh, he's got a hard-on!" To ease his angriness, I end up having sex with him. Kind of weird. [Laughs.] The hairy suit thing was just—there was hair stuck on me, and it was everywhere. That was definitely the weirdest scene I've done.

How would you describe your fans?

I wouldn't say there's a general word or phrase to explain them all. For the most part, all of my fans have been amazing. I guess the non-fans are the ones that are angry and stuff like that. All of my fans have been really amazing. I feel like a lot of them just really appreciate the fact that I take the time to respond to my e-mail personally, and I try to get back to as many of them as possible. I asked around when I started my website, and I was like, "What should I have on my website?" A lot of people asked for a blog. A lot of people like to watch my scenes and videos, but they also enjoy getting to know me a little more. I guess it's what you call a little more of the girlfriend experience.

You mentioned the non-fans being angry. What do you mean by that?

Everyone in this profession gets hate mail. I really think I've angered the Asian community. They are going to see this and get angry. I'm not ashamed to say I'm 100-percent Chinese. I was born in China, and I speak Mandarin, and I went to a Chinese school. I guess that really angers the Asian community, because they're like, "You have no right affiliating yourself with us." But I can't help my nationality. I can't help my upbringing. So, a lot of angry people like that. There are, of course, people that are religious, and "You're going to go to hell for what you do," and there are just some people who are angry that I do porn in general. I always think it's a little weird, because I'm like, "How did you find my e-mail? You took all this time to look me up and find my e-mail. How do you even know who I am?" Watch a little porn…

What effect does that kind of negativity have on you?

It always hurts, but I think I've learned to handle it. People saying really, really mean things, I think, affected me more when I first started. Like there are some forums where there are entire pages dedicated to bashing me. I'm not going to read it. You know what? I don't need to know what these people are saying, because it's nothing constructive. It's just talking crap. I learned to really let it go. No matter what you do, there's always going to be somebody who doesn't agree with it.

What are your professional goals, both on- and off-screen?

For off-screen, I definitely hope to do something related to public relations in the future. I've always loved that. Public relations can make a bad situation better. For porn, I would love to shoot a feature film before I get out. The idea of a real story, a real script, a way bigger set—it's not going to be just a couch and fucking. It's going to be a story.

If you had a daughter and she wanted to enter the adult film industry, what you say to her?

I know this is going to be pretty hypocritical, but nobody—I don't think *anybody*, whether they do it themselves or not, would want their kid to do it. I mean, I would say that I've done things in my life that I wouldn't ever want my kids to do. I had sex at 17, but if I had a daughter, I'd be like, "You know what, wait until you get married." Okay, it wouldn't be until you get married. "Wait until you're like twenty-something, okay? Please?" I know that I wouldn't be, "Oh, yeah, I've gotten a 'D' in school." I'd be like, "I was a straight-A student. You better be that way, too." Everyone always, I guess, had higher goals and expectations for their children than they do for themselves. They always want their kids to maybe be better than themselves. If she did end up doing porn, I wouldn't be so against it, but if she hadn't started yet and said, "Hey, do you think I should do this?" I would say, "You know what, I personally think there are other options." I really do believe that. I think I wouldn't have gone through a lot of the crap I've had to go through if I didn't do porn. If I was just a model, per se, I wouldn't have all these people being angry, calling me a "whore" or whatever.

Have you ever been in a situation where you were embarrassed by what you do for a living?

Yeah, I would definitely say so. It's mostly when I talk to friends or people from high school. You know, like people from high school message me, and say "Hey, I saw that video with you and the Yeti." It's kind of a "Wow-I-can't-believe-you-did-that" kind of thing.

Have you ever felt like you were being taken advantage of?

When I first started the industry, like I said, I was working with a photographer whom I trusted, and he wanted to act as my agent at that time. Since I didn't know how to go about getting into the porn industry, I said, "Okay." All he did was post my information and my pictures on a modeling website. People actually just contacted him, and he pretended to be me. I guess the people he was dealing with had no idea they were talking to him and not me. He wanted 25-percent, which is way above industry standard for an agent fee. So, after I talked to some of the people on set on my second day, they were like, "That's kind of ridiculous." I remember he was like, "Oh, we have to do practice scenes." I was like, "Okaaaay, sure." It kind of make sense, I guess. He was like, "I have to have footage to show the companies that want to hire you." I guess I really did feel taken advantage of. Whenever a girl messages about getting into the industry, I have an FAQ on my website, which also says "If you have any questions, please just ask me. I don't want anyone else to get taken advantage of." I understand a lot of these girls just turned 18, and haven't really been out there in the world for themselves, so they're gullible and vulnerable.

How about on-set?

On-set, not really. I would say on-set, if you ever feel like something is going the way you don't like, or you are not comfortable with it, you can pretty much say, "No." I think I've been pretty lucky on-set. I've never had something I was absolutely against where they were like, "Nope, you've got to do it."

MARI POSSA

EL SALVADORIAN IMPORT MIRNA GRANADOS first found work in the adult film industry as a receptionist for Seymore, Inc. After working at that job for three years, she was then promoted to porn star/mogul Seymore Butts' personal assistant. Having gotten a firsthand look at the porn industry, the attractive 5'2" Latina decided she wanted to work in front of the camera under the stage name Mari Possa. According to Possa, her reasoning for changing careers was simple: "[It was] the thrill, the excitement, the money, the fame—it was all of it. It is my way of being free of any inhibitions. I love sex, I love watching people have sex, I love watching me have sex."

Seymore Butts, who would later become Possa's offscreen love interest, served as her mentor in the porn industry. Not wanting to see her quickly burn out the way many new starlets do, he gradually eased her into the business. She began with solo masturbation scenes and then worked her way up to boy-girl scenes with Butts himself. Because Possa's decision to enter the business coincided with the filming of Butts' reality television series *Family Business*, the series chronicled her earliest days as a porn star, which included everything from breast augmentation to the selection of her porn name.

Because of her appearances on that series coupled with her unabashed enjoyment of what she does—her porn specialty is anal sex—Mari Possa has become one of the biggest names in porn.

KEY PORN TITLES: *It's Raining Tushy Girls*, *Tongue in Cheeks*, and *Jamaican Me Horny*.

MAINSTREAM CRED: Mari Possa appeared in thirty-seven episodes of the popular Showtime series *Family Business*.

Mari Possa is one of the hottest actresses working in the adult film business. Photograph by Greg Hadel courtesy of Mari Possa.

How would you describe your childhood?

I would describe my childhood as being a happy one—a sheltered one. My grandma tried to shelter us. I grew up basically with my grandma. I lived here in the states and then in El Salvador for five years.

Was your family religious?

My grandma is very religious. My parents aren't, but we tried to go to church once with them when we were younger. But when we became teenagers, it was over for us. We were old enough that we could say, "No, I don't want to go to church." [Laughs.]

What kind of student were you?

I'd say I was a good student up until the seventh grade. Then, after I discovered boys, it all went downhill from there. When I was in high school, school was probably the last thing on my mind. I just went boy crazy. All I wanted to do was socialize with the boys.

How did you end up working for Adam Glasser, a.k.a. Seymore Butts?

I was living in New York for three months. Then winter came, so I decided to move back to California. I was working for a lawyer, and I wasn't happy. I felt that I was doing all his work, and he wasn't paying me as much as I thought I deserved. So I was looking for another job, and someone told me to look in the newspaper, and I did. As I'm going through the classifieds, I came across an ad for an entertainment company. I was like, "Oh, entertainment company!" So I sent in my resume. They interviewed me and she said, "Do you want to see what kind of movies we make here?" So they took me to the warehouse, and I saw some of Adam's stuff. I was like, "Oh, my goodness." Up until that point, the only porn I had seen was Vivid. Then I saw Adam's—even his box covers are hardcore. [Laughs.] But I wasn't scared. I took the job, because I was so unhappy working for the lawyer's office.

What were your thoughts on porn prior to going to work for Adam?

At that time, I just thought porn was Vivid, because that was basically all I had ever seen. My boyfriends and I used to watch it. Not all the time, you know... I had seen some porn, but it wasn't hardcore or anything. So I was a little naïve about it. [Laughs.]

What made you decide to become a porn actress, and was this something you'd been considering for a while?

I contemplated the idea of working in the adult film industry for about a year before I finally took the plunge. I mean, I've never had a problem with nudity. I was working for Adam, working on the *Tushy Girl* magazine. Every time I saw one of the pictures in the magazine I would think, "I want to be one of the girls in this magazine." I didn't see anything wrong with it. At that time, I was dating and having sex, so the only difference now is that I'm being filmed while I have sex.

So I thought about the idea for a year, because I knew it was something that my family was not going to be happy with if I actually did it. They knew I was already working for an adult film company, and that alone was an "I can't believe you work there, blah, blah, blah" type thing. I knew if I decided to do anything in porn, it was going to cause some drama in my family, so I thought about it for a long time. After that, I realized that it was my life—not my parents'. So I started by sending my pictures in to Playboy TV, and they called me up to do one of their shows, *The Sexy Girl Next Door*. And then I did some other shows. So I was like, "You know what? I'm going to do the movies." I felt I was ready for it, so I told Adam. At first he didn't think I was serious—he thought I was joking. And I said, "Nooo!" And he told me I should think about it. And I said, "I've been thinking about it for a year now." So that's how I got into the adult film industry.

Did you discuss this decision with your family or friends?

I didn't discuss it with them. I thought about everything, and knowing what they were going to say, I thought, "You know what? It won't make any difference if I tell them before or after I do the movies. Either way, I'm going to hear the same drama from them." So, being that I'm a brat and I usually do what I want, I told them after. But the thing was, I think my dad was watching the Playboy Channel. And I was living with my parents. And my dad would get the mail and I'd get letters from Playboy TV, right? It would have the little logo on it and he'd say, "This is for you, my little Playboy girl? What is this?" And he came across one of the shows while watching Playboy. He saw it and asked my mom, "Did you know she was doing Playboy TV?" At this point I was already doing the adult stuff, but they thought it was only Playboy TV. My mom was like, "There's nothing wrong with that. It's not like she's having sex. It's all pretend stuff." And so she came up to me, and that's when I told her. I said, "Well, you know what? That was a few months ago, and now I'm doing movies." They couldn't believe it. My sister, she's like my best friend, had a hard time, because I didn't tell her about it. She cried for several hours. I said, "This is what I want to do with my life. Sorry if it bothers you."

Now they're over it. It worked out in the end for me. They still think I'm crazy. They're like, "She's gonna do what she wants." Don't we all, though?

Your entrance into the adult film industry was captured on the Showtime reality series Family Business. *How did this show affect your career and personal life?*

As far as my career, I'd say it put me on the map more than any of the girls that do porn, because the show got to play in Italy and Europe—all over the world. So I have fans all over the place, and to me, that's great. It helped my career a lot. I also think it gave my family a little more sense of what I'm doing. And it portrayed the industry in a good way. In a sense, I think it made my family worry a little bit less about me.

What was your first porn set like?

My first porn set was at my boss' house at the time. [Laughs.] At Adam's house. It was a house I was familiar with. I wasn't surprised or anything. I mean, I had been in the industry behind the scenes, so I just had to be in front of the camera this time.

Were you nervous?

Yeah, I would say I was a little nervous. I tried to prepare myself. I think it would be a little abnormal if I wasn't nervous. So yeah, I was a little apprehensive about it, but like everything else, I just went for it.

How beneficial was it knowing Adam before filming?

It was very beneficial. It made me feel a little bit more comfortable. In a way, I knew he wasn't going to shoot me in a way that would make me look bad. I also knew he'd let me know if there was anything I needed to be doing differently. It wasn't like he was directing me, but more like he was helping me out. I was very comfortable.

Are there any adult scenes you would like to do, but haven't yet?

Yeah, I would like to do a gangbang. No kidding. But you know what? In the short time I've worked in adult film, I'd have to say that I think I've done about everything I've ever wanted to do. I mean, there may be something I haven't thought of yet...

What's the best thing about being a porn star?

I think it's the time it allows you to do other things. Shooting a scene—I guess it depends, because if you're shooting gonzo, which is mainly what I do—it's only like five hours. Then you have the rest of the day to yourself. The time it allows you to do other stuff is definitely an upside.

What's the worst thing about being a porn star?

The main thing is obviously the STDs. I mean, if there were no STDs, I think we'd have a lot more porn people out there, right? [Laughs.]

If you had a daughter who wanted to enter the adult film industry, would you let her, knowing what you know?

Would I let my daughter enter the business? I'd have to say no, because it's not as glamorous as people think it is. I'd have to say no.

What's the oddest set experience you've had?

I won't say any names, but I worked with this one guy who had a curved penis. This wasn't the first time I've been with a guy who had a curved penis, but we were doing reverse cowgirl anal, so it just kind of felt like he was scratching my back instead. [Laughs.] It was funny actually.

Do you do anything onscreen that you don't do in real life?

Yes, there's a lot of stuff I do onscreen that I don't do in real life. Like facials—what is *that* about? Do people really do that? You know, it's a lot of stuff that's not conventional that I did just for the scene—just for the viewer.

If you had not become a porn star, where do you think you'd be now?

I think I would maybe be a real estate agent or a teacher. You know, something in an office…something ordinary.

There are several adult toys with your name and face on them now. How did these come about, and how do you feel about them?

I'm very happy with my toy line. And I have Seymore to thank for that. He just made it all possible for me. He came up to me with the idea, and I said, "Yeah, sure. Why not? Who doesn't want their own toy line?"

Do you get feedback on the toys?

Yes. I get e-mails about them, so my vibrating ass is very popular out there. [Laughs.]

How has your life changed since becoming an adult film star?

Maybe I haven't changed, I think, because I still have all the friends I used to have. The only thing that has changed is people knowing who I am—being exposed to more people.

When you and Adam go out, are the two of you recognized?

He's recognized all over the place. It's crazy, and in the weirdest places. At night, just walking down a dark street… "Seymore Butts! We've seen your TV show!" We're like, "Oh, my goodness. You can see us?" He gets recognized the most. I think if they recognize me they don't really come up to me. For instance, I just received an email from a guy that I take my car to… Obviously, he didn't say anything, but then he'll send me an email. "Hey, I saw you at the dealer…" Why didn't you say hello then? I think they're a little bit intimidated. I don't understand it. I mean, that's why I do it…for the attention…for the men out there.

What kind of fan mail do you receive?

Oh, my goodness. Crazy fan mail for me. I just got one from a virgin who is twenty-four-years-old, and obviously, he thinks I'm the hottest thing ever. He knows I'm a porn star, and he wants me to take his virginity. But he wants us to tape it also. He wants us to put it on video. [Laughs.] He thinks it's going to help my career! Oh, it's so funny, stuff like that. A lot of people—men mostly—tell me how beautiful I am. I get some very nice compliments. The good thing is that I don't get hate mail. People would think that. I mean, a lot of the girls get stuff from church, but I don't get any of that. I'm lucky in that way.

What's the strangest encounter you've ever had with a fan?

This guy came to a signing at a bookstore and just wouldn't go away. He's taking pictures, and then more pictures. And I was like, "There's only so many pictures you can take, right?" But he kept snapping away. He even ran out of film, went and bought more, and came back to take more pictures. I was like, Oh, my God. I was a little bit scared. I think that was the strangest. Other than that, the strangest encounters would be at the conventions. People want to grab you. Just because you're a porn star, you're free to let anyone touch you, I guess.

Do fans ever give you gifts?

Yes. I have a number one fan, I have to say. Everyone says they're your number one fan, but there's this one guy... He's always sending me stuff, which is so cute. He sends me stuff like little cards, poems, flowers... One time he sent me money in the mail. I know it's cute, but it's like, dude, come on.

Do you have any regrets?

No, I don't think I have any regrets. I try to live my life like, whatever I did wrong today, forget about it. We're all human—we all make mistakes. So I'm not going to dwell on it, you know? So I've made mistakes, but I don't really regret them. I feel that they help me grow as a person.

LINDA ROBERTS

LINDA ROBERTS was born in 1957 in New York, New York. She worked in theatre and later found some success in "B" movies such as *The Summoned* alongside actors Robert Z' Dar and Joe Estevez and *The Flesh Merchant* starring Margo Romero and Estevez. Roberts' husband, Frank Castle, was a successful adult film director. Considering that they were real-life swingers who enjoyed photographing and videotaping their private sex life, it was probably inevitable that Linda Roberts would embark upon a career in the adult film industry. The only surprise? That Roberts didn't embark upon this career until she was thirty-eight-years-old.

Roberts and hubby Frank started out by sending photographs to a variety of adult publications. When literally every single publication that they contacted purchased her photographs, it quickly became apparent that she had real potential in the industry. Roberts, along with her husband, began making her own homegrown pornography and then worked her way up the industry ladder from there. Roberts has since become a staple in the MILF genre and has appeared in more than 100 films. In 2007, *The New Neighbors*, a film on which Roberts and her husband collaborated, received an impressive eight *Adult Video News* Awards nominations. These included Best Video Feature, as well as Best Director (Castle) and Best Actress (Roberts) nominations. The film also received the *Night Moves* Editor's Choice Award for Best Feature.

KEY PORN TITLES: *My Friend's Hot Mom #10*, *Cougar Recruit*, and *The New Neighbors*.

MAINSTREAM CRED: Before entering the adult film world, Linda Roberts appeared in a handful of "B" thrillers.

New York native Linda Roberts has made a name for herself as one of the biggest stars of the MILF genre. Photograph courtesy of Linda Roberts.

Tell me about your childhood.

What most people looking from the outside in would say is we were kind of like *Leave it to Beaver*. I'm the oldest out of six. I have two younger sisters and three younger brothers. We grew up in Queens, New York. When I was about seven, we moved out to Westchester County, which is more like suburbia. We were just normal kids. We played stickball and football in the backyard. Our house was always the congregating place. My parents were always involved in all our activities. I went to elementary and high school in Westchester. When I was about eight, I started taking dance lessons. Actually, my dance teacher lived across the street from us, so I was never around. I was always taking classes or whatever. When I got into my older teens, I started doing Summer Stock, and she would bring me on the shows she was doing. Eventually, I started assistant choreographing shows. That was sort of my main thing, go to school or go to dance class. That's what I did mostly. I did that for many years. It was all the normal things. I was a twirler in band. We did fire batons, the whole thing. It was just normal, being a kid in the sixties. And then for my senior year, I lived in Holland as an exchange student with a Dutch family. That was truly an amazing, eye opening experience for me. We're still very close to this day. It went on like that. It was normal Middle America, really, although living near a big city, which is a little unusual, but no sign that I would ever end up doing adult.

What were your parents' attitudes towards sex when you were growing up?

Well, they had six kids, so clearly sex was not an issue at all. And everything at our house... I remember, and people laugh at this story, but my brothers were in their teens, and Dad always had a stack of *Playboy* magazines or whatever around next to other magazines he read. It was just always around. My brothers were starting to get into watching adult videos. My brother rented, I want to say it was *Debbie Does Dallas*—the original. In the end, the entire family ended up sitting around watching it, which I'm sure totally ruined the experience for him and probably scarred him for life on some level. [Laughs.] It was in a room that we called the library; it had a TV, bookshelves filled with books and stuff... I remember looking around the library at stuff and just going, "This is so fucking weird." So, it was pretty open. It wasn't like we were a hippie commune. It was there, it was open. When you have six kids, sex is something you just sort of accept as normal because, well, how else did I get here unless you have other beliefs in virgin births and stuff. As many families would have their kids believe.

Do you consider yourself an exhibitionist?

I don't consider myself one, per se. But by the same token, because of all the years I spent doing theatre, and being onstage, and even more so backstage, you just get comfortable with that crap, or you just don't survive. And it's really interesting, because it sounds like it's not a big deal, but being able to do that comfortable is really a skill. It's something you can't develop. If you don't have that innately, you can't go on to the next steps. You're not going to be able to do that. Like I said, I think exhibitionism, to me, is more of a tease thing where somebody is going to flash or whatever just to get the reaction. I mean, they're truly comfortable, but there's a different aspect to it. It's different than being in adult. It's exhibitionism on one level, but on another level, not all exhibitionists can actually have hardcore sex on-camera or be on-camera being naked. So I think there's two different skills going on there, whatever they may be.

What sort of student were you?

Straight A's. Goodie two shoes. Never missed a class. I don't think I ever missed a day of school. Actually, I think I missed about four days of school in all the years of school; something like that—it was ridiculous. I was just one of those goodie two shoes. It was really hard on my brothers and sisters. When the oldest comes through and all the teachers are just, you know, raving about your older sister, then you don't want to have to keep up those standards. It gets really difficult.

Did you have any interest in pornography before entering the adult film industry?

I'd seen some, but I never really thought about it. I never thought, "Oh, I want to be a stripper." I never thought, "Oh, I want to be an adult actress." It really never even dawned on me. I should say the only time that it crossed my field of vision was when I was auditioning for stuff on Broadway. At the time, the big show in New York was *Oh! Calcutta!*, which had been running for years and years and years. Of course, in that show there are a lot of nude scenes. And they needed dancers who would be on stage and be comfortable being naked. So that was the only time I ever really considered it.

You didn't start making adult films until you were in your late-thirties. What made you decide to get into porn at that point?

I was actually thirty-eight when I started. It was on a dare, more or less. My husband had been after me for a long time to do some photo shoots, and basically my thought at that point was, "Nobody's going to want to see these pictures. This is just stupid." But we had been filming ourselves for about six years. Taking pictures—he has photo albums full of stuff. I finally thought, "Oh screw it. I'm just going to prove him wrong." I'm going to do this, and we're going to send it out to a few magazines, and it's just going to fall flat, and it won't happen, and then he'll get off my case. Well, that wasn't what happened. The photos were bought by everyone we sent them to. The rest is just kind of history.

Do you feel that it's been a harder road for you because of your age?

Actually, I was very fortunate, because about the time that I started out was when they were transitioning into the whole MILF genre. So the reality is that at that point, there was way more of a gap. In some ways. Although thirty-five-year-olds were getting more work, it was a different type of gap. The young girls worked from like eighteen or twenty to mid-thirties. Then that's kind of where it fell apart. Nowadays, it's like if you're twenty-five, you're already over the hill. Until you hit about thirty-five, and then you can do your MILF stuff. Because I was so much older and there weren't a lot of people doing it, it was more of a pure field. It was truly women who were older. I think it was actually beneficial to me. If I had been twenty-five, I would have been heading into the end age range at that point. It would have been harder on some level, so it was actually easier for me at that point.

What does your family think about your working in the adult film industry?

I don't think most of them know. I haven't sat down and said, "Hey, by the way, I'm an adult star." My parents know that we have an adult production company. I'm sure they suspect or guess. My family is cool in the sense that they won't really care one way or another. There will be some raised brows. There might be some people outside of my direct family that might be offended or whatever. For the most part, my family is kind of like, "Do whatever you're going to do." For a while, I was going back and forth to Florida to do some work in Miami. My parents lived just north of there, so they'd come down and have dinner with me or whatever. But I keep it separate. There's no need to put it in front of people, unless they really want to know about it. It's just never really come up. We're out here, totally removed from it. It is what it is.

Your husband is among the directors on the adult films you've done. Does that make it awkward for your or your costars?

It never has for me. It's almost easier in some ways. I know a lot of couples have a lot of trouble with that. I'm not sure that I understand why it's so difficult, but I guess there's a jealousy factor for them. He doesn't have that jealousy factor. So for me, it's actually a little comforting, because I know already going in who I'm dealing with. You take one big risk factor out of there, so you can focus on other things. And I like when he's not directing, if he can come to the shoots with me, because I don't have to worry about the periphery stuff. It just cuts down on the number of times you get bothered on the set or whatever might come up. Although, honestly, that's not such a huge issue. I haven't found it to be. I guess maybe if I were eighteen to twenty, that'd be a thing to worry about. For older women, I think the guys are a little more respectful. I may be wrong about that, but that's how I see it.

Has it had any effect on your relationship, good or bad?

For us, it's just a part of our lives. We've been photographing ourselves or taping ourselves or whatever for many years, so it's just a part of who we are. I would say it's definitely not been negative in terms that we've already worked out all the jealousy issues that can come up. We're past that.

What does it take to be a successful adult film actress?

That's a hard one, because I think there are so many levels here. One is age range. What does it take to be a successful eighteen to twenty-year-old in the business right now? I wouldn't wish it on anybody, because they become so manipulated by agencies, and a lot of these girls forced to do things they don't want to do, and they don't know better, and they don't know enough about their bodies, about the way things are supposed to be. They're told, "Yeah, yeah, that's okay. Whatever." And they're getting hurt. They're getting used up really fast. They're just commodities to most of these guys. In terms of that, I think it takes a really tough kid to brazen it out. I think the older women, like Nina Hartley who was part of that original group of people who created the industry, for her to be a success is a whole different ball of wax as well. She just keeps doing it, because she's really good at it, and she really enjoys it, obviously. For the rest of us, I'm not sure what it takes. I mean, the look is part of it. Getting one good film was a big part of it. Where the film got promoted, and there was a PR team behind us, and they got my name out there, got me on the search engines and that stuff. My stuff started getting noticed a little bit, and honestly today the internet is a huge part because once upon a time we had to count on every film we were in getting foreign distribution. If it gets distributed here, fine, whatever, but the foreign market was always big, and my market to a large degree is overseas. Now with stuff going on the Internet and with having a MySpace page or whatever, I get emails from young kids sometimes all over the world. It's a little scary because sixteen-year-olds in Italy are sending e-mails that have seen my stuff. It's like, "Okay, that's not really the way it's supposed to be."

Do you have rules for your male costars?

I try not to. I have things I don't do. I have a couple of guys that I won't work with ever. I try really to go into it without any preconceived stuff. Biggest rule for me is that I want to have a good time, because if we're not having fun having sex, then nobody's going to want to watch whatever we're doing. I don't want to be…basically, I'm not your bitch. I don't want to be slapped around. If we're doing a fetish thing, that's a whole different thing. And I don't do that as a normal part of what I shoot. They basically just treat me with respect. It makes the scenes a little easier.

But I gather from what I've seen recently on set with the guys that some of these girls have a lot of rules. I actually had a scene where a guy was having trouble getting hard. He was trying stuff, and nothing was happening, so I said, "Would you like help?" And he just looked at me like, "Okay, nobody does that anymore. You'd be willing to do that?" "Okay, we're in this scene together, and wouldn't it be better if I helped you, because then we would have this connection going, and then it might make the scene a little easier?" I just got the weirdest look from him like he was surprised I would do it. I was like, "What is going on out there?" I find it really hard to believe, because once upon a time that was the norm. That is not the norm anymore. It's just weird to me that the girls are so… From what I've heard from other people who are out there with the other girls, it's pretty bad out there.

How frequently are your on-camera orgasms real and how often would you say they're fake?

Once upon a time, when we were shooting our own stuff, which we're trying to get back into and when we were working with some of the older stars or names that are not really in the business anymore, I always had a real orgasm. *Always* real. And now, the way they're shooting, and the guys that are out there, who started to believe they are the stars of the scene as opposed to the female in the scene with them, rarely anymore. Which is really too bad. I mean, it really is too bad. Most of the guys out there, I'm sorry, cannot fuck. And the guys who are doing the shooting, that's not what they're looking for. Patrick Collins at Elegant Angel has an entire line of that. She has to come, whatever you have to do to make her come. It doesn't have to look pretty, and it doesn't have to be facing the camera; there's no rules, just whatever makes it look the best. I think that's just a really brilliant idea because it's not done anymore. I think you can tell when it's not real. If I hear one more girl "ooh aaah" through her scene because she's so clearly not enjoying it... I just think that comes across, and that's not what the fans want to see. There may be a percentage of fans that kind of want to see that, but I think the vast majority of fans want to see the real thing, and I want to see two people who really look like they're having fun fucking, and if that's not coming across then I don't know. I just don't think that's what porn is supposed to be about. Unfortunately, I feel that's all that porn is about. It makes a challenge for me in wanting to do this.

Are you a sexual person off-screen?

Generally, yes. I don't think you could do this if you weren't. Although, funny you should say that. But, yes, I'm sexual, and that's one of the things that led us to get into doing adult. You know, it was just our way of expressing it, I think. It's fun. I think what's fun about it, which at the same time is a drawback, is that you get to have sex with a lot of different people with no strings, no anything. At the same time, it's hard to have sex with people you don't have a connection with, because your body needs that connection. So it's sort of a weird thing, but it's a nice little outlet because, like I said, you get to have sex with people you normally wouldn't get to fuck.

Which is easier for you: the dialogue or the sex?

I can do both. I don't have an issue with either one.

Because you have a theatre background.

Yeah, I have a background in theatre. And I can do really good off-the-cuff ad-lib dialogue, which a lot of them don't like to do. And I did get nominated for a best actress award for an AVN in 2007. Obviously, I can do it. I think I just bring something else to it. If the scenarios are dumb or whatever, but you can have some fun with it. I had a guy shooting a scene and for whatever reason, I still don't understand why they wanted so much—usually the dialogue is maybe a minute or two—but this guy needed fifteen minutes of dialogue. I'm thinking, "That's a lot of dialogue." And so he played opposite me behind the camera—you never see him, you just hear his voice—and he's following me around with the camera. We ad-libbed fifteen minutes in one take. He was just absolutely blown away. He's like, "I've never seen that done before." The problem for me is that once I do it, I can't replace it, I can't repeat it. If you've ever done dialogue with Ron Jeremy, he can go back to the beginning and repeat everything he just said verbatim. It's unbelievable. I can't do that. Working with him is really challenging for me, because I really have to be on my toes. But I like that. I like working with somebody who's so into doing the dialogue and can do it so freely, but so many people out there just have such limited skills with that.

I did a feature for Metro that I had turned down at first, because I didn't have enough time to learn the dialogue that was a quite a few pages. It was for a friend of mine who is a director, and he went away, and they said they really wanted me to do it, and he came back and said he was going to change the schedule so I'd have time to learn it. The other person in the scene with me ended up never opening the script until the day she walked on set. It wasn't like she was a great Academy Award-winning actress; she could barely read the lines. What we literally did is two lines of her, lines of me so she could learn the script. He shot it that way. It was excruciating. I don't know what the final film looked like, because I never bothered to watch it, knowing it was going to be awful. At the same time, I was brought back to do a scene, because something had happened. They brought me in to do a scene with Ron Jeremy. I've done a ton of scenes with Ron Jeremy that are just straight dialogue, and that's just really fun. Then you're doing it with someone who's good at it, and it's fun. He's funny, the energy level is high, and it was just such a pleasure. What a difference.

You've done quite a few MILF films. Are you worried about being typecast?

I'm already typecast. I'm fifty-one. There ain't no going back. [Laughs.] The reality is that I'm already pushed into the next category, which they're now calling GILF. Yes, grannies doing sex. I'm not real keen on that. I was having enough trouble with MILF. The only reason I'm concerned about typecasting is, personally, I don't like the genre that much. A MILF, right, technically you can be 21 and have a child and be a MILF. That's not what the actual meaning of it is supposed to be. So we ran out of forty- year-olds, so we just expanded it to be anybody with a child is a MILF. No, not really. I think that's bothering me more than anything. Personally, in my private life, I don't think. Being forced to do a scene with a guy who's playing eighteen or whatever, I can take that or leave it. I would much rather do a scene with a hot older guy. Give me Randy Spears any day. I'm sorry, but that's the truth. There's a sexy older guy, and he's so much sexier than any of the young guys out there that I know of or that I've worked with. It's amazing. These guys are just walking through it, because they don't like older women. So for them, it's not a turn on either. "I can at least pretend," but you have to hold up your end of it. It's hard. I really am careful about what I take. I want to be careful who I work with. It's a tough situation. You can't go back, though. I won't be twenty-two again. Unfortunately.

How do most of your roles come about?

For a long time, most of our early stuff was we shot scenes for our own production company. And we sold them homegrown. They sold their catalog to Adam and Eve. In their catalog, I'm in like half the scenes on there. So it's really pretty amazing. And then there's word of mouth. Friends who are big directors. And then some guy called me, and he's been a fan for a long time, and is starting a website, and wanted me to shoot some stills for him, so I'm doing that tomorrow. So I get that kind of call. I have a listing on SexyJobs, and I get a lot of calls from that. A lot of those jobs don't pan out. But it's mostly just word of mouth; people have seen me and know my stuff.

Do you enjoy watching yourself have sex in your films?

No. I never watch my films. *Never.* I don't care if it's straight stuff or adult. I hate it, and I won't do it.

What kinds of things does an adult film star worry about while the cameras are rolling?

Oh, God, that's so much. Worry about his position, how it looks, how they're lighting it, how the make up is, how your hair looks, everything. It really depends on the person. I really don't have to worry about those things. I think the older you get, probably the more that is a concern of yours. Either that or you go totally the other way and go, "Fuck it, I'm old. Who cares?" But, honestly, I've always gone into it thinking, "I have to look my best—how are those lights looking?" And the older you get, the harder it is for that to maintain, and to end up showing up on set that day looking the way you are—there's a lot going on. And then there's always five minutes of that position; five minutes this position; being a mental clock on how long you need, and remembering to look at the camera and get signals if they need you to do something; there's a ton of stuff going on.

Are there any sex acts you have or would refuse to do?

I don't do anal. *Ever.* I do gangbangs, but you said sex acts, which, to me, is different than an orgy or multiple guys. It's an intent thing more than anything. I don't do fetish stuff on camera at the moment. I have friends who are big into the fetish community, so at some point I might do some of that, but because I'm not big on the fetish, I'm still at the putting my toes in the water sort of place. I still have to explore it. I don't do slapping, spitting—those things I won't do either. If that ever came up, I'd get up and walk off the set. Be done. That's pretty much it. I'm pretty easygoing. As long as I'm not getting hurt, I'm probably okay with it.

Who are some of your favorite actors to work with, and why?

Randy Spears. There's a reason to me that he's the top guy in the business. I love Mike Horner. He's just amazingly talented. He and Randy both have the ability to do dialogue and sex scenes well. Kyle Stone is a longtime favorite of mine. We've worked together a lot. I haven't worked with him in a long time. He's older, I'm older, we're not allowed to work together, apparently. I like the older guys. Of the younger crew, I liked working with Jack Venice. He's a nice kid. I really enjoyed him. Most of the guys are okay; no one's really sticking out in my head going, "Name me! Name me!" There's been a couple that I would not work with again. I've been pretty lucky, I guess.

You took some time off from doing adult films at one point. Why was that?

We did a big feature called *The New Neighbors*. It was very successful. It was funded by an eccentric millionaire who, right as the film was about to be nominated for eight awards, kind of just pulled the rug out from under us. We continued on promoting it on our own, with no backing from him for a year. Got through the awards, but we were expecting that we would have picked up a couple of awards, but because he pulled his advertising and stuff, we didn't get anything, and we were very upset by that. I was really pissed off and not happy with the way that played out. I just got to the point that I had decided that I didn't want to continue on. It happens in mainstream a lot. But you get it out there, and you do a great job, you promote the hell out of it, you do everything right, except for the person who's supposed to be distributing it or financing it or whatever just ruins whatever chance you have to parlay that in to something. And I really had to decide whether I wanted to continue. I figured that was my shot for getting into features, and after that it was going to be mostly, "Did I want to go back to Gonzo?" I really didn't. I did go back to Gonzo because I wanted to get my name back out there a little bit for a while.

What's the oddest experience you've ever had onset?

It wasn't actually while we were shooting that day, but the guy who owned the location had gotten really drunk, and then he got really crazy, and he started threatening to kill us. He kicked us out of the location. My husband, Frank, was the director, and he went back in to talk to this guy. I actually grabbed a gun in case this guy started shooting. That was kind of a strange night. He wouldn't let us get our equipment, get our stuff out. We still had stuff to shoot there. It was insane. I'd say that was our strangest encounter.

Do you have any desire to direct?

I shot and sort of directed since we have our own company. I haven't done a lot. Actually, it'd be kind of fun to direct a little bit. Gonzo sort of directs itself, though. I don't know if I'm up to directing a whole feature. It takes a skill set. You need to know what you're doing. I'm not sure that I have enough knowledge; especially stuff involving the camera, that side of it. If it came along and I had the opportunity, I would love to do it.

What are your professional goals?

In terms of adult, it's hard to say goals for me, because I'm in my fifties. I'm kind of winding down. I guess I'm going to ride the wave as long as it's out there—as long as I feel like I can put my body on camera and still look halfway decent. Overall, my career is winding down, and there's no question about it. I'm not really excited about being grandma on-camera, so I may be at the borderline of needing to wrap this up pretty soon. So, long-term goals, not really any.

If a female came to you for advice and was considering entering the adult film industry, what would you tell her?

I think women really need to examine their motives for doing it. It seems a lot more glamorous than it is. I think especially when you come in, and you're young. You don't have your shit together, and if you're coming in for the wrong reasons, you will get eaten alive. This industry is really full of guys who hate women. I hate to say that, but it's true. You have to be really tough to put yourself out there with that overriding attitude. Especially with young girls, because there are lots of times they are made to do scenes that are going to physically harm them, where they're going to get torn up; literally torn up. You need to know your body, and you need to know when to go to the hospital. Stuff like that sounds really disgusting, but they need to ask themselves, "Am I familiar with this stuff?" Do you know enough about your body to know what is right and what is wrong for you? Are you tough enough to stand up and say I can't do that scene, that's just not going to work for me?

Older women, I think it's a whole other thing. It's more, "Are you comfortable putting yourself out on camera naked for the world to see at forty-whatever?" If you're good with that, hey, go for it. It's fun. Most of what you see is someone comes in for a scene or two, and then they're gone, because it's hard work. It really is. You're not always going to get an orgasm. You're not always going to be treated as well. It's mostly about taking them aside and saying, "Are you sure this is what you really want to do? Are you prepared for most people in mainstream looking down on what you do? It's going to be really hard to find a relationship with a guy."

What do you see as being the future of the adult film industry?

It's sure changing, that's for sure. It's hard to say, because I think they're destroying the few niches that were really successful. They killed MILF, and now they're working on killing Cougar. Young girl stuff is always going to be popular, because we're a society of pedophiles. Sorry, but it's true. I'm hoping it gets back to the point where girls twenty-eight to thirty-five still have careers. You're losing a whole big talent pool by only liking young girls or older women. Everyone talks about there being no DVD sales, it's all internet. I really disagree. Yes, DVD sales are down. However, in relationship to the fact that there's so many people shooting this crap and nobody's stuff was selling…the sales are probably down a little bit. We're basically seeing the people that were bad shooters, making absolute shit, being forced out of the industry, which I don't think is a bad thing.

I read an interesting article that surveyed baby boomers. They do not want to watch their porn on the internet. They will go out and buy it. So, when I hear this gloom and doom about DVD sales, yeah, the nature of it is changing, but if you make good product and get it promoted properly, you will still sell it. The key is you have to make good product, and I think there are very few people out there making good product, and there hasn't been for a very long time. You can't just slap it together and think people are going to buy it. They are way more sophisticated these days. The other people are downloading and watching it on their cell phones, God knows why. That's the nature of that market, and yes, they are internet-based. If you try to get that market then, yes, you need to be on the Internet. If it's something they want and it's good, they are going to buy it on DVD. Too many people out there don't care about what they're putting out; it's just product. Getting product, getting product, getting product… You know what? The distributors screwed us all that way. They just kept clamoring for product. They didn't really need product. They need to sell more copies of the movies they already have. So instead, they kept saying, "Oh, we need more product." Then, all of the sudden, there'd be 1,200 things a week out. Then you're selling two copies, because who can have 1,200 pieces of merchandise? I think we took a page out of mainstream, and it really killed the industry. To a large degree, that more than anything hurt us. Greed, it always screws everything up.

Are you seeing any trends that disturb you?

I'm kind of an "if-somebody-wants-to-see-it, somebody-will-make-it" kind of person. But some of that really extreme crap that's being done—I'm sorry, it's crap. It's not helpful in a society that already has a lot of issues about how people treat each other to see people beating each other up. If you're doing a pure, full-on fetish thing, and everybody knows that they're watching a fetish thing, and people are into this, I'm okay with that. There's other stuff where it's a lot more degrading and a lot less pleasant. I'm not sure if it qualifies as obscene and should be prosecuted, and at the same time, I'm not sure I really want to watch it. Or that it's of any help to society that it's being made. I've heard it referred to as "circus acts." Do we really need to make it into "circus acts?" It's already clear that people have issues with sex, and it's being portrayed in ways that are less than stellar. To make it into "circus acts" maybe takes it down a few more notches. And it hurts us all, because this industry is looked down on anyway, and then as an industry, we're lumped in with the guy making "circus act" films. There's no need for bestiality. Not on *any* level. *Ever.* End of discussion.

Do you think men and women look for different things in an adult film?

Absolutely. I think they look for a lot of the same things, but something a single guy might watch is different than a single female. It's different than a gay female or gay male. What couples look for together is completely different than the above. I think the underlying thing is that they want to see great sex; people having fun. On both sides of that, I think they're less concerned with how people look and more for how the overall feel of the video is. If everybody is having a good time, but the actors are a little average, people are still going to want to watch it. Guys are still going to buy it. I think the more average the guy, the more the guys are going to like it because they can picture themselves, a "picture-your-dick-here" kind of thing. They relate better to certain male talent who aren't ripped with six packs or whatever. I think the same thing probably goes for women. I think guys tend to look more at the women and less at the guy. I think women will look more at both. I think overall that as long as you're making good videos, everyone will want to watch them. That's just the bottom line.

Have you ever been in a situation where you found yourself embarrassed by what you do for a living?

Not embarrassed, but I did have a situation come up recently. Outside of my adult life, I'm a graphic artist. I had gone on an interview. I had a really great meeting with these people and spent three hours with them. Everything was all great. We were going to start working together in a few weeks. I didn't hear anything. I contacted her and never heard back. That's really weird, but maybe there's a problem with the e-mail. I e-mailed her again. She had inadvertently found out about what I do. She was horrifically offended. She could hardly bring herself to write the e-mail to me. She said, "You're going to have to be more careful about this if you're worried about people finding out." I e-mailed her back and said, "Frankly, I'm not that worried about people finding out. I don't have any problem with what I do. If I did, I wouldn't be doing it. My only problem is that I'm upset you were so offended by it. It would never be my goal to offend somebody by what I do in my personal life. I thought it was interesting, and something maybe you want to think about, but when you didn't know you didn't have an issue with me. You thought I was a nice person, and you wanted to work with me. What changed? I do something in my personal life that has nothing to do with working for you. Why should it be such a concern for you? Why should you be so offended by it?"

Obviously if I was a school teacher, my personal life...well that wouldn't work. I fully understand that. We're both adults here. We're both over the age of consent. We both know what goes on in the real world. I never forced it on her; she found out inadvertently. I have plenty of clients whom it never comes up for. I have other clients who know what I do. They're all cool with it; we're adults here. Nobody questions it. For me, it was okay because the job wasn't paying anywhere near my rate. I also didn't want to put myself in the position of being around someone who'd be uncomfortable. The people surrounding me even outside of adult life who know or suspect, it's all good. Nobody cares. Nobody asks. They're just accepting of who you are.

KYLE STONE

KYLE STONE was discovered by porn starlet Nasty Natasha in 1992 while working at a prestigious Century City law firm. Stone kept his job at the law firm while working nights and weekends in porn for three years. Stone worked often, amassing an impressive number of film credits, and his work would eventually be seen by his coworkers on the Spice Channel. This led to the circulation of rumors within the office, and then, one of the firm's secretaries was screening his films daily for his coworkers. Soon, one of Stone's coworkers—the same secretary who had been organizing screenings of his films—started complaining about working in the same office with a porn star. "She could play it off like it was all disgusting to her," he has said. "If it was so disgusting, why was she making an effort to go get it? That bothered me. If it bothers you, don't watch it. You can change the channel or not rent the tape. I'm not forcing it on people." Predictably, Stone was soon fired from his day job because of his night job.

After working first with director Rodney Moore alongside his mentor Nasty Natasha, Stone has, to date, amassed more than 1,500 film credits. In 2007, he was inducted into the *Adult Video News* Hall of Fame after working for 15 years in the industry. Today, Stone continues to work in the industry, often playing the role of the funny guy or the older male, but he has seen his workload greatly diminished because of the impact of Viagra on the porn world. As the ever-reliable Stone is fond of saying, "What once was a skill is now a pill."

KEY PORN TITLES: *Safari Jane, Natural Born Thrillers,* and *Alice in Analand.*

What was your childhood like?

I was kind of a nerdy kid. Growing up, I had a tough time. I was literally suicidal for a time. It was the typical thing; you know, the world's against you, all this weird shit. And then one day, I just turned everything around and decided that was it. I was a good person. I liked me, and I decided that if nobody else did, then to hell with them.

Having appeared in more than 1,500 films, adult film star Kyle Stone is considered a living legend. Photograph courtesy of Kyle Stone.

I grew up in Santa Monica. This is my hometown we're sitting in here. I've been here all my life. Not a bad life growing up on the beach. I had my growing pains like everyone else, but I managed to make it this far, so I guess I'm doing all right.

I was a horny child. That horniness began when I was about five years old. I used to hump furniture. I didn't know what I was doing, but I just knew that it felt good. I used to go to class in elementary school, and I would lean against my desk and press my penis up against it. Once again, I didn't know what I was doing. Nobody ever told me. Then one of my teachers stopped me one time. She said, "I know what you're doing feels good, but there's a time and a place for certain things, and school is not one of them." Her name was Miss Baker, and she gave me a gold star for every day that I didn't do that in class. She kind of explained to me what it was all about, and what I was doing. My parents were extremely Catholic, so they didn't know what was going on.

I saw porn and I thought about what a great job that would be. And then I ended up in it years and years later.

What were your parents' attitudes towards sex?

They were extremely Catholic, and they didn't talk about it. My father was Irish. My mother was Italian. They didn't discuss sex or anything like that. It was something that was ever brought up. Like I said, I had the problem that I had, and they didn't want to talk about it. I was actually very fortunate to grow up with a mother, father, and grandmother, all living in the house. I had three brothers; a total of seven of us in the house. Most of my friends' parents were divorced, so I was one of the few kids who actually had both parents living at home. There was nothing unusual. Neither of my parents was violent. My dad was a bit of an alcoholic. I guess he did get a little bit violent towards my older brother, but I avoided it, because every time I heard my father get upset, school was always the main reason. I made sure that I went to school and did well, and as long as I did well in school, I could pretty much do whatever I wanted.

I started smoking weed at a young age. My older brother was a little bit of an influence there. But I used it to my advantage. If I wanted to smoke out, I had to get all my homework done first. So I used that as a motivator. "If I get all my homework finished, I can go party." It worked out well. I had a 3.52 GPA.

One day I remember my dad giving my younger brother a whole lot of trouble. He started to get a little violent—he was never *too* violent, though. He started to get close to what I thought was too much, so I stepped up to him. I said, "Dad, back off." He grabbed me, and pushed me up against the wall, and said, "That's for you!" I just looked at him and said, "What?" I knew he didn't have anything. He said, "Uh, duh, um…nothing." Because I was doing fine in school. I was getting As and Bs, so what could he say? He says, "I don't want you smoking that pot." I said, "Why not?" He didn't have an argument with me, so he pretty much let me go. He didn't have much to say. I wasn't abused. Most people think everyone in this industry was abused, but no, not really. Some of us are just perverted.

That would be me. [Laughs.]

When did you have your first sexual experience?

I was very young. I found out that by lying on the floor and pressing my pelvis to it, I could create a sensation down there that felt really good. Like I said, five years old. I don't think I was ejaculating, but I was getting a sensation with no other way of getting it. I didn't know how I discovered it, but yeah, five or six years old would have been my first sexual experience.

As far as having sex with a girl, that was different… That didn't happen until I was 13 or 14; somewhere around there. I remember it was with my first girlfriend. I acted like I knew what I was doing, even though I had no clue. She was a virgin, so this was the blind leading the blind.

There's a famous story about how you got into the porn industry. Tell me about that.

Well, there was a girl that I used to talk to on the phone. We would have phone sex. That was all it was, and it wasn't something that we did a lot. You know, every once in a while, and I hadn't talked to her in almost a year. She had moved away, and that's why we talked on the phone. One day, I decided to call her. I dialed the number, and a girl answered. I said, "Hey, how's it going? It's me." She says, "Who's me?" I said, "Sydney?" She went, "No, this is Natasha." So I apologized and told her that I must have had the wrong number. She then asked me what number I was trying to dial, and I told her. "Well," she said, "you dialed the right number, but there's no Sydney here." "What number were you trying to dial?" she asked. So I told her. She said, "Well, you dialed the right number, but there's no Sydney here." I said, "Oh, well, I'm sorry." She goes, "You haven't talked to Sydney in quite some time, have you?" I said, "No, it's been almost a year." She said, "Yeah, cause I just got this phone number today." She says, "What were you going to talk to Sydney about?" I hemmed and hawed and didn't want to answer the question. She said, "You're calling a woman at one in the morning and you don't know what you want to talk about? You were going to talk about sex, weren't you?" I said, "Well, the thought had crossed my mind." She says, "Well, tell me what you were going to say." I said no, because I knew I could get into trouble for that. I said, "I could go to jail for that because I don't know you. I'm not going to say anything." She tries to tell me it's okay, and I'm like, "So you say, and then the police show up... I'll tell you what. I'll give you my phone number, and you can call me back, and I'll tell you anything you want." I knew that if someone calls you, you can say anything you want to them, and you can't be held responsible. So I gave her my number, and she called back, and we had phone sex.

Afterwards, she said, "Guess what I do for a living?" I said, "Phone sex operator?" She says, "No, I do porn for a living." I was like, "Yeah, right," and she said, "No, really I do." I didn't believe her. Then she starts saying she's in this movie and that movie. She says to go out and check them out. So I went and got a couple of the movies. I put it in and the voice was exactly the same. She had a very distinct voice. I'm looking at it, and this girl was *hot*. She went by Naughty Natasha. I looked her up and can't find any pictures of her now, but she's the one who got me into the industry. We ended up meeting a couple of weeks after that. And then, a few weeks after our first meeting, we ended up getting together and having sex. And as soon as we were done she said, "Ever thought about being in the industry?" I said, "Let's see, I'm an American male, I've seen porn... Uh, yeah. Pretty much every guy has, yeah." Then she said, "I think you could do it if you wanted to." So I guess she saw raw potential there. I said yes, and she said, "Not so fast." I said, "That figures." She was smart. She said, "I want you to think about this and wait a week. You've got to think about the ramifications. I have a feeling you're going to be good at this, and you could even become famous for it. People might recognize you. Your family could find out. People you work with could find out. You've got to be able to deal with that, so go home and think about it first." And I did.

Man, I'm glad she had me do that. Anybody reading this book and thinking about getting into the industry, take the time to seriously consider all the ramifications, because even though you think you have them all covered, there are going to be things that are going to happen. It happened to me. A girl I was dating before I got into this industry, she had moved back to New Jersey... I talked to her on the phone, and I thought she knew. I was wrong. She freaked out. "Don't ever tell anyone we even dated!" I said, "Darling, I got into this business after you, okay?" She didn't want anything to do with me; she didn't want to talk to me ever again. From this girl, totally unexpected. But that's what happens. You just never know.

Why have you stayed in porn?

I was a natural. I liked it. It was something that I really enjoyed. I was comfortable. I liked the acting. It's funny, because my mother, once she found out, asked me I why I didn't just pursue acting. I didn't know I liked acting until I got into this industry. I didn't know I was any good at it either. It was after I got in and did a few things, and I had people coming up to me saying, "You are such a great actor." I'm literally turning around to see who they are talking to. There's nobody back there. Finally, I got it into my head that they were talking to me.

Have you ever considered trying to go mainstream?

Of course. I've met a few people who are in the industry who have seen my work, and there has been a little talk about them slipping me into a couple of things. I've had a couple of directors say they'd consider it, but nothing's ever panned out. They're all afraid. What I think will eventually happen is somebody will put me in a mainstream movie without knowing who I am first. Just a small little bit part. And then, before the movie comes out, leak that somehow an adult film star snuck into the movie. It's like, gee, I wonder what kind of publicity that would create. It's funny, because I have tried to get some work going, and I'm always being told I'm such a great actor, but I have such a hard time getting anyone to give me a shot. A lot of the movies they shoot for Showtime, Cinemax... I tried to get into a few of those, but I don't have the physical attributes. I'm not tall enough. I'm more on the pale side even though I go to the tanning place to get color on me. And I don't have six-pack abs or any of that. I'm just the average guy, which is part of my appeal.

A lot of people have told me that the love of sex is the primary reason they stay in porn. For others it's financial reasons.

That's the thing. I was doing wonderfully financially. That's why I'm a little bitter. But I had found a career that I loved, that I was very good at, that I got paid really well for. And that was just like the best job I could possibly have. Period. End of story. And that job was taken away from me not by people who were better than me, but by people that had access to medication that made them better than me. And it happened at a time that I was just hitting a stride. I was doing a lot of feature work. I was getting scripts everyday. I was getting to do a lot of acting. I was having a lot of fun. Then the pill came out, and in a three-week period, my work load got cut in half. Not many people I know of could have their income cut in half and still survive. But that's what happened, it literally got cut in half. I kept getting less and less work, because more and more people were coming into the industry.

Once the pill took over, *everything* changed. Literally, they could get any guy they wanted. That's when my career, and all the careers of the porn guys I know, started to drop, and we had to start looking for other things to do, because now there were all these new guys who were all in their twenties. They all think they are the greatest things in the world, but if we took their little pills away from them, they wouldn't be able to do our jobs, now would they? I stayed because I was a natural at it, loved it, and thought it was fun. It was just the perfect job for me. And unfortunately, it got taken from me.

That's basically what happened. And the dynamics about everything in the industry have completely changed. Girls, they've changed. The scenes have changed. All the guys have changed. Standards have changed. It used to be sexy. Now it's a circus act. Everything's a circus act. How many dicks can we shove into this girl? How many can we get her to stick in her mouth? Everything has gone that point now. I don't like it as much as I used to. I used to defend the industry, but I can't defend it anymore. Back when I started, we needed the girl. The girl was very important. When she walked on set, she was treated like a queen—from the moment she got there to the moment she left. She was always treated like royalty. This was because you needed her to have the best possible attitude and the best emotional situation she could be in, because if she wasn't happy, she wasn't going to help the male talent. If she didn't cooperate, it was going to be a long day. However, since the pill, I've heard directors say, "Where's the whore? Get that whore in here! Where's that whore?" You would never have heard a director say stuff like that before, no way. You don't want to insult the girl. They don't care anymore; she could be crying, but they wouldn't care. Why? It no longer matters, because her behavior is not going to affect the wood. Today, the wood is there before she is.

What would you say is an advantage to being in adult films?

I don't know that there is an advantage. I really wouldn't put it that way. There are definitely more disadvantages.

What would you say are the disadvantages?

A lot of doors get shut. Maybe not as overtly as they used to, but they're still being shut. Also, the girls have changed. In 1992 when I started there were 25 guys. There was an average of 25 guys in the industry up until '98, '99. That's all there was, 25 of us. A couple would come, a couple would go, but on average 25 guys would be working all the time. When people would say, "How come I see the same few guys?," it was because there were only so many of us who could do it. It was a very closed crew. Now I'm guessing there are probably close to 150 guys in the industry. Or 200. I would not be surprised if there were 200 guys in the industry right now. That's a big increase.

The other thing is, the girls have all changed. When I was in the business, the average age of the girls was, say, 24 to 32. Now the average age is 19. Once again, big change. The pill is part of that, too. The pill allowed these younger and better looking guys to come in, which enticed more younger girls to come in because the guys are better looking. The girls would also come in because they all think they're going to be the next Jenna Jameson. That's not going to happen. Jenna Jameson was a bad marketing move. She was created by some ingenious marketing over at Wicked Pictures. Jenna is very intelligent, very smart. She knew what she was doing, knew how to play the game. She did everything right. She was not stupid about it. The thing is, they built Jenna into this big thing, and then she left Wicked and went to their main competitor, Vivid. She was over there a couple of years, and then she leaves Vivid and creates her own company called Club Jenna. Club Jenna was in direct competition with what two companies? Wicked and Vivid. Everyone else in the industry sat around and went, "That wasn't too bright, now was it?" Building up that girl really backfired. They created their own competition. You haven't heard of that anymore since then, have you? They'll get to a certain point now, and they'll cut them. They don't build them up like they used to.

People look at me like I'm crazy and I'll say, "Well, how come in the mid-Nineties if you went down Sunset Boulevard, you would see billboards with the Vivid and others' girls on them?" You don't see those anymore. They don't want to promote them. The promotion over the huge starlet is over. Jenna was the last one. The only time it's going to happen now is if one of these girls self-promotes themselves. It's got to be a self-promotion thing, and there's going to be people in the industry who are going to try to squash it. They all see the *E! True Hollywood Story* on Jenna Jameson, and I guarantee after that runs, we get flooded from girls coming from all over the country. I would love if someone would do a study that [shows that] when they air that around the country how many more girls flood into our industry. I saw one time that in two weeks there were more girls in the industry than two weeks before.

When you're on the set, what's your regular routine?

Usually I find the director and let him know I'm there. I try to find out where they are in the shoot. Depending on whether it's a feature or not, whether I have lines or not, then I try to concentrate on that. Find out what scenes are up. Study my work. A lot of times I will try to find the girl I'm working with if I'm doing a sex scene, introduce myself, say hello. If it's somebody I worked with before, okay, no big deal, just say hello. If it's somebody I've never worked with before—I got criticized occasionally for this, but it's something I wanted to do—I would ask the girl about her likes and dislikes. I would like to know what she really liked to have done to her, and what she definitely did not want to have done to her. The reason I always did this is because I figured that first of all, the scenes are about her. The theme of every scene I ever did is more her, less me. If I'm watching it, I want to see more her and less me. The less they see of me, the better the scene.

The other thing is, I want the girl to have as much fun and enjoy the scene as much as possible, because that shows. So I want to have everything she likes be done to her, and I don't want to anything that she doesn't want to have done to her. So the likes and dislikes are always very important. I also found out by doing that how the scene was probably going to go. That's the other thing. The girls today are all 18- and 19-years-old. So you go up to them and say, "So what do you like and dislike?" "Oh, whatever…" As soon as you hear that, you know one thing—the girl has no idea what even makes her come. She doesn't. If you were to ask an older woman—one of the girls who had been in the business a while like when I first started—she would say, "Don't do this, don't do this, but do this and this, and if you really want to get me off, do this, this, this, and as soon as you hear me make this noise, do that." I mean they'd literally give you the step by step. Those scenes rocked. She's in tune with what she likes, and you've now tuned yourself into what she wants. The two of you can now work together to make shit happen, because it's all about her having a great time. The new girls are all like, "Whatever, uh huh. I'm 18, I'm here." No, they don't know. They haven't had enough experience.

One of the things that happened, it was a blow job. Brand new girl. Scene started. I dropped my pants. I wasn't hard. She looked at me like there was something wrong. She got a look of panic, eyes all bugged out. She says, "You're not hard." I said no. "But you're not hard." I said no. "They've always been hard." I started laughing, and said, "First of all, every guy that you were with back home in the back seat was so happy to be getting any pussy that he was rock hard before you touched him. Apparently all the guys that you've been working with since you got in the business have all been taking pills, so they were all hard before you even touched them." She starts, "Yeah, they've always been hard. I mean, like, hard." "Yeah, honey, that's because you had nothing to do with it." I said, " Go ahead and grab it and touch it." So she put her hands on me, and I asked her to look up at me. Just from doing that, I started to get hard. You hear, "Whoa!" I said, "What?" "It's getting hard." I said, "Yeah. It's not only doing that, it's doing it just for you." She loved that concept. Apparently it had never happened to her before. She realized she had an influence over what was going on with me. It was apparently an awakening for her. She got a big kick out of it. It was fun after that. She got me hard, and I rocked, she started blowing me, and the scene went beautifully. But I was the first guy that she had ever gotten hard. And my guess is that if she's still in the business, probably the last one, which is sad because I've actually had people stop me—fans— and I always get the same thing. Fans stop me and they say, "Where can I buy some old porn?" They all want old porn. They want stuff from the Nineties, the early to mid-'90's, my golden years. And I always ask why, and lately I've been getting the same answer. One guy will say, "I just want to watch something where the girl's not spit on, slapped, choked, made to cry, doesn't gag or tear up. Just a normal scene." And I laugh. A couple of guys stopped me, and say, "My thing is I like to watch the girl get the guy hard." And I started laughing and said, "Dude, you're shit out of luck." He says, "What do you mean?" I go, "They won't shoot that anymore." He says, "What are you talking about?" I go, "Directors will not shoot the guy un- less it's coming out of his pants like this." They say, "Why? The hottest part of all the scenes was watching the girl get the guy hard." I say, "I agree with you a hundred and fifty percent, but they don't shoot it anymore. Girls don't even know what a soft penis is anymore. They've never seen it. They don't know what to do with it. They're insulted. Literally, they get insulted if it's that way. This is what we've come to as a country.

Do you do anything special to keep it hard for that long of a period?

I've always been able to perform. All the old school guys, all the guys before '98—you were in the industry, and you worked a lot. We all had one thing in common. We all loved women. Seriously, *loved* women. I'm sure there are people out there right now going, "Well, duh, all the guys in porn do." No, they don't. You watch the current stuff, watch some of these guys have sex—they don't like women. You can see how they're taking all their aggressions out. First of all, they have an appendage now that she has no influence on. She can't make it go away. She can cry, scream, throw a tantrum, throw up—she can do anything she wants, but it's not going away.

So these guys use it like a weapon. I watch these guys, and it's literally pound, pound, pound... I'm like, "You really don't like women, do you? Did you not have a good relationship with your mother? What is the problem here, dude? Are you trying to get back at every woman who ever said a bad thing about you? What is the problem?" I mean, the way they choke these women... Now, I like rough sex. Rough sex is fine. But every time you have sex, it has to be that aggressive and that rough? If that's the case, then there's something wrong. I prefer a nice, romantic, kissing, touching, caressing, you know, hot scene. I've worked with girls on some scenes lately, and this last girl was like, "I don't really like guys to force me down and do the gagging thing." I'm like, "Darlin', I'm old school. I will give you a hard penis, and you can do with it what you want. That's what we used to do. We'd get it up, we'd lay back, and you'd take it. You'd go down as far as you wanted. I might put my hand on the back of your head, but I'm not going to put any pressure on you. My hand's going to move, and your head's going to move with it. It may look like it to the untrained eye who's watching. It may look like I am, but you're doing the movements, not me. I'm not pressuring you to go deeper, none of that stuff. I put my hand on the back of your head, and you move your head, and my hand stays with it. That's all. I don't force."

There's this thing called tapping out, and that's brand new. It came along with the Viagra thing. What's happening now is you have the girl deep throat them, and as soon as she's got it all the way down her throat, you grab her head and hold it against your pelvis. Now she's got an appendage down her throat. She obviously can't breathe. And you hold her there until she taps your leg, and then you let her off. Usually at that point, she's either choking, gagging, throwing up, or all of the above. First time I saw this, I almost died. I could not believe I saw what I was seeing. If I had tried that back in my day—and remember, this girl almost threw up, had tears streaming down her face, and the crew high-fived the guy. Back in my day, had I tried something like that, two things would happen. Number one, she would probably bite down, and then I'd scream and push her off. Then when everyone came around and said, "What happened?" The girl would say, "That motherfucker was holding my head down on his cock and wouldn't let me up, and I couldn't breathe." At that point, the crew and the rest of the male cast would have beat the shit out of me. I would have gotten my ass kicked. Literally, *beat down*. "How dare you do that to a female talent, you motherfucker!" *Bam, bam, bam*, and deservedly so. I would have gotten a beat down. Now, if I do the same thing today I get high fives. Okay, that's wrong. That's just wrong. That's the typical mentality the pill has brought to the industry. As far as I'm concerned, the pill has brought every negative connotation that was there before, and actually brought it all to life. The fact that people say, "Oh, that's really degrading to women." Well, I didn't think so before. I would literally stand up for it. I'd say, "Degrading, my ass. You come see how we treat that girl. You would *love* to be that girl. She's treated like a friggin' princess." Of course, back then the sex scenes weren't circus acts. There wasn't any degradation there. Now I can't say that. There's a lot of degradation. *Lots* of it.

And what's this thing where every girl over 23 is suddenly a MILF? If you don't have "teen" in your age, you're a MILF now. No. MILFs are early- to late- thirties to forties, okay? You cannot be a MILF at 23. Sorry, I don't care how many kids you have. It doesn't work that way. In our industry now, if you're not 19—even if you're 20—you're a MILF.

If you had the ability to do so, what changes would you make in the adult film industry?

I'd outlaw Viagra and all the erectile dysfunction drugs. I was talking to somebody the other day, and I said, "You know, if you really want to come up with a movie that would be a money-making opportunity is to do an old school one." The hard part would be convincing the guys, but I actually thought of a way of doing it. What we need to do is start a company called O.S.P. Call it Old School Porn. And shoot old school porn, which means when the guy takes his pants off, he's not hard. And I was talking to this guy about it, and he says, "Well, how would we do that?" I go, "Simple. You tell him to take the pill right as the scene starts." It'll take about half an hour to kick in. Once it gets hard, it'll stay that way. The thing about our industry is that people always want what they can't get. Right now, that's what you can't get. All you can get is circus acts. How many blow bangs or girls surrounded by five guys can we get? Some of these scenarios I've been in are just ridiculous. A guy and a girl will have sex. As soon as they're done, the girl will be laying there going, "Oh, that was so hot, I just wish I had a little more." The guy will go, "Oh, no problem." Five of his buddies come out *naked* from another room. Why are five guys in another room naked? But they come in, and she does a blow bang with these five guys. Literally, there are five guys in the other room just hanging out naked. Okay. That's what I mean. If you were to do something like a guy and a girl on a couch like they used to do in the old days… They have *sex*. Nothing freaky. Popshot, it's over. I think people would like it. I don't know that I can convince anybody to make it, but I think it would sell.

What has been your favorite scene, and why?

I don't know that I have any one particular scene that I consider to be my favorite. I've done a lot of great scenes. I did a scene with Racquel Divine on a little prop plane. We were flying along the coast here, from Malibu to the marina. That was a blast. Just her and I in the backseat. The pilot kept turning around and watching. I said, "Dude, we'll get you a copy. Just fly the plane." Things like that were memorable. They took me to the Philippines for a movie. That was a great experience. I did a scene with a blonde, a brunette, and a redhead—that was pretty trippy. That was good.

Something that goes along the lines of that are my favorite performers. Kylie Ireland has a special spot in my heart. My mother passed away one day in February of 1999, and that day, I was scheduled to work with Kylie. They had my mother on life support, and she had all but died. By that evening, it was over. I was at the hospital, and I knew I had to be on set. I didn't know what to do, and my father said, "What's the problem?" I said, "Well, I'm supposed to work today, but mom's here, and I don't know what to do." He said, "What do you think your mother would say?" "Mom would say if you're not a doctor, you're not going to do me any good at the hospital, so go to work." He said, "Then go to work." So I went. I got there, and obviously I was not in my right mind. Or didn't look like I normally looked. So everyone kept asking, "What's wrong?" So I told them, and the director and Kylie, Chloe, Nicole, were basically saying, "Get out of here." I said, "There's really nothing for me there. I would just be staring at the walls. At least here I have something to do." I stayed, and I did the scene. What I say about it is that I don't remember the scene at all, which is really kind of strange. I remember it starting, and I remember it being over, but I don't remember anything specific about the scene. I don't know what positions we did, how long it went. I just know that on the worst day of my life, Kylie allowed me to go to a happy place for about an hour and a half, and she took over. I didn't have to think about what was going on in my life, which was the worst moment I had ever had. For about two hours, she allowed me to get away from it. That meant a great, great deal to me. I don't know what would have happened to me if I hadn't had that opportunity and that situation the way it was. Some people say it's weird, but it helped me. *Misspelled* is the name of the movie, and I've never seen it. I have no idea how that scene came out, but that was an important day.

Did you notice any changes in yourself once you started doing porn?

I don't really know. I would like to think I didn't change a whole lot. I don't know that that's necessarily accurate. I started to feel a little more confident in regards to my acting and my performing. This is what surprises me, all the guys back when I was working—we worked a lot, okay? But I don't think any of us had an attitude like we were the shit. You know what I mean? And that's what I laugh about now, because I see these guys now on set that are all taking a pill to do the job, and they strut around like they are the hottest fucking things in the world. These guys, "I'm a porn star, and I'm fucking these hot chicks." And I'm like, "Big fucking deal. Nobody's buying the movie for you, dude." We all knew what our place was. We were meat puppets. We're filler. The girls are the stars. We're just lucky enough to be part of it. Just helping out the scene. None of us walked around with an attitude. If you compare the two jobs, we had the right to walk around with that attitude because we were really doing the work. We had skill. All these guys now strut around like they're the biggest shit. I'm like, "Dude, if the pharmaceutical companies shut down tomorrow, you won't work next week, and you know it. So drop the fucking attitude." But they don't. They walk around, "I'm the shit, I'm the shit." "No, you're not. If I take your pill away, you couldn't fuck your way out of a paper bag."

What advice would you give a man who wants to enter the adult film industry?

I would tell them not to. Be a porn star in your own home. If you get into the business now, you are going to be required to take E.D. drugs. I don't give a shit what you say; you are required to take E.D. drugs. Because if you go on-set, and she pulls your pants down, and it doesn't pop out like it's been set in a cast, if it's not rock-hard and ready to go, they're not calling you again. You won't work. One of the reasons they don't want to hire me anymore is that they know I want to be a natural performer, and they don't want to take that chance that I might not be able to do it. Let's see, 16 years and 1,500 movies, and you still think I'm going to fail? Okay, whatever.

Do you feel the industry is more difficult for a man or a woman?

For a woman, no doubt. Especially now. All those attitudes I was talking about earlier? Where do you think they take them all out on? So the girls are going to be *pounded*; stretched; brutalized. There's no other way of putting it. I would love to sit here and go, "It's all just flowers and wonderful times." But no, it's brutal. Friggin' brutal. And that's one of the things that bugs me. They make every girl the same. Sasha Grey, when she first got in the business, was phenomenal at group sex. Her and gangbang stuff. She could handle eight guys easily. And she would make it look good. The problem is she doesn't stand out, because they make all the girls do it whether they want to or not. Whether they have the capability of handling it or not doesn't matter, they just throw them in there. That doesn't allow a girl like Sasha to stand out, because they make them all do it, whereas if they hadn't made all those other girls do all that crap, girls like Sasha would stand out. I'm talking about the brutality of the scenes. It's pound, pound, pound, pound, pound. Even when the scene doesn't call for it.

A director friend of mine was talking about this guy who's in the industry who is known for one thing—he fucks at one speed, a million miles an hour. The director is having to direct him in a scene that was calling for it to be romantic. That's what the scene called for. He went to the guy and says, "It's got to be romantic." The guy gets in there and starts going a million miles an hour right away, pounding. The director calls cut. He takes the male talent off to the side and says, "Listen, this is supposed to be a very romantic scene, and I want you to go in there and caress her, kiss her. Slowly, not a million miles an hour." Guy gets back in there, and starts going the same speed. Director calls cut, says, "Dude, I want you to…" The guy looks at the director and says, "Look, man, you're cramping my style." Without missing a beat the director says, "Dude, that's not style." He didn't get it. He was incapable of doing anything but that one speed—that rabbit fucking! That's the problem with a lot of these guys: they have no concept of anything else. You take that hard penis, and you pound on that pussy until the girl cries. That's the way it works now.

What kinds of things factor into your decision of whether or not to make a film?

Usually just what they want me to do. If you look into my credits, you'll see I'm listed under one bi-sexual movie. I was in a bi movie. People go, "Oh my God," but it's no big deal. He calls me up one day and says "I really like your acting, and think you're really good. I've got a part that I want you to play. I'm doing a bi movie…" I went, "Whoa, hold on." He says, "Now, listen. The scene is going to be you and a black guy who was a part of the other side of the business. You and the girl are going to be playing prison guards. She's going to be fucking this guy with a strap-on. You're going to come up behind the girl, Anita, and fuck her while she fucks him." And I said, "Okay," and that's what we did. The guy never touched me, and I never touched him. No big deal. Didn't bother me. I don't care. It went fine. I want to know what they want me to do, and if I'm comfortable with it, then fine.

I'll give you an example: Tom Byron called me up one day and said, "Look, we're doing this big movie, and I want you to play a prince." I say, "Sure, no problem." He says, "Well, there's a little bit of a catch. When the scene opens up, the camera is going to pan across the room to you sitting on a throne. It's going to look like there's a young boy between your legs simulating giving you a blow job. Then when the scene starts, you push him away and you begin this long speech." I said, "Okay." He says, "Are you okay with that?" I say, "Sure." He says, "You don't mind?" And I say, "No. Of course not. It's going to be simulated, and he's not actually going to touch me, so what do I care? What's the worst that's going to happen, people think I'm gay? It makes me a great actor, because I'm not, so what do I care? If people think that, then I consider it great acting. No big deal." I would have actually done the thing, but it was a big deal—one of the few sets I've actually walked off of. Basically they asked me to be there at seven o'clock in the morning for a call time, which is unheard of. I got there at seven, and no one was there, so I went home. They called me at 11, and said, "Come on back." I never did.

Coming up for Wicked, Jonathan Morgan has me doing a non-sex role. I'm playing a gay counselor. I don't care. I love the acting. If I can convince people that I'm a certain way, then that means my acting is good. So I don't really care. I know who I am. I'm very comfortable with who I am sexually.

What was it like getting inducted into the AVN Hall of Fame?

It was the worst night of my life. They treated me like dirt. The one night of my life that I was really looking forward to turned out to be the only time that I've ever really felt ashamed of being in the industry. They gave me seats as far back as you could possibly go in the auditorium; I was one row from the back wall. If I had gone to the row behind me and leaned back, I would have hit the wall. The stage was here, and I was way the fuck back there. On the night that I was inducted into the Hall of Fame! They called me on-set and told me they were going to induct me into the Hall of Fame in January. "We would like to know if you'd like to attend." "Absolutely. Okay." Rick Masters was also inducted that night. I had never won an award. Not one, period. This was the one award where you actually knew the award you were going to get was the Hall of Hame award. It wasn't something that had to be voted on. They were decided in November, so if you were on that list, you were getting the award. It wasn't like you were in a category, and one person out of six was going to win.

They always had those awards made up, and in January, after the show, you'd go backstage, and they'd give it to you, and as you walked out, you got pictures taken by the paparazzi with you holding the award. That makes sense, right? It was a beautiful thing. So I decide since I've never had an award, and this is going to be the first time, and it's going to be for the Hall of Fame on top of everything else, I had a friend of mine make me a suit. It cost me over $500, and the whole idea was that it was going to be something special that I could show. It was a total Vegas jacket, studs and all that. So I had this suit made up, and I go there, and we get onto the convention floor, and we get to the AVN booth. They take us into this nice little conference thing and sit us down, saying, "Oh, yeah, Hall of Fame. Here are your tickets. Okay, good." I have my girlfriend with me. Rick has some people with him. We get our tickets, never bothering to question where they were. They knew who they were giving the tickets to, and they knew we were in the Hall of Fame, so we figured everything was good. We just took the tickets.

So the night of the show comes, and we go down there, and there's a paparazzi line. I try to get in on it. "I'm Kyle Stone. I'm being inducted into the Hall of Fame." They are excited, and wanting to take photos. Gene Simmons is in front of me, further up on the paparazzi line. What the fuck Gene Simmons is doing there, I don't know. But everyone's taking pictures of him. As soon as I'm getting up to where the paparazzi is, someone comes up, "Shut it off, we're running late." They start shutting off all the lights. So a couple of paparazzi start trying to take some pictures of me as the lights are going off. I don't know if any of those pictures ever came out, but I doubt it. Okay, whatever. So I go inside. Where are these seats? Oh, they're that way. Finally, I found out where these seats are. I found out later they were literally in a section they call the 'throwaway section.' Okay, these were the throwaway seats. Me and my fellow Hall of Fame inductees were put in throwaway seats! We're in with the regular crowd. AVN, you cannot put porn girls in with civilians. You cannot do it. But they did. Some of the girls were getting propositioned by all these fuckheads around us, "How much for a blow job up here in the stands?" Like that's what the girls want to hear on a night like this. Sure, great stuff.

Then an announcement is made: "No awards will be given out this evening. If you are a recipient of an award this evening, it will be mailed to your residence in three or four weeks' time." I'm thinking they're just talking about the regular awards. There's no way they're talking about the Hall of Fame awards. They make those up early, I know. I'll go find someone and ask. I couldn't find anyone from AVN, but I found another guy who was inducted into the Hall of Fame that year. "Where do we pick up our award?" He says, "We don't." So I say, "What do you mean we don't?" "I just asked so and so from AVN, and they don't have them." I'm like, "They always have the Hall of Fame awards." He goes, "Not this year. They're going to mail them to us." "Well," I say, "what are we supposed to have our pictures taken with?" And he says, "You don't." So I'm upset. "I'm not going to have a Hall of Fame award to walk out of here with?" And he goes, "Nope."

Really? So now I'm 15 shades of pissed. I spent way too much money on this suit, my girlfriend paid for the hotel, I've been waiting my whole career for this, and then they put me in these cheap-ass fucking seats! I can't even see the stage. And then I find out that I'm not going to get an award on top of all that? The award show goes off, I don't even watch it. I wound up going out into the hallway, and ran into hundreds of fans, and just sat there talking to them. A couple of them found out how pissed I was, and they bought me drinks and stuff like that. I had a good time just sitting with the fans, but I was pissed. The night ended, and I didn't get an award. I've got nothing to show for that night. Three months later, I go to AVN and picked up my award because I didn't trust them to mail it to me. I picked it up from the office, brought it home, and sat it up on my mantle in the box; I didn't even take it out of the box. I left it in there for another month. I didn't even want to take it out. I was that pissed off. I took pictures of it in the box. Finally, I took it out and sat it on the mantle with the ticket stub as to where I sat so you could see it.

I plan to have a nice picture taken of me holding it, and it's going to say, "This is the only picture in existence of me holding this award. Period." There's no other picture *anywhere*, and there should be. There should be a lot of them. But they took that away from us, too.

I was ashamed. I had never been ashamed of what I did before. At that moment, on the one night when I should not have felt any shame, I was totally ashamed of who and what I was. It was one of the saddest moments in my career, and it shouldn't have been. And AVN knew what they had done. I made it very clear to them how much they had fucked me over. I told them all. I figured maybe if they were smart they'd invite me and V.I.P. me for 2008, and they'd make sure I'd get treated especially well. It wouldn't make up for my award, but I didn't really expect that. But I expected them to at least make an effort to at least do something. But they didn't even call me. And the worst thing about the entire night was that they gave Gene Simmons a Golden Tongue Award. And as I sat there in my seat, so far back, two questions popped into my mind. One, if you had the time and energy to have that Golden Tongue Award made up, then why the hell couldn't you have taken the time to make up the Hall of Fame awards for the people who have actually put the time into this industry? And secondly, why the fuck was Gene Simmons getting a Golden Tongue Award? How many movies has his tongue been in in the porn industry? Let me think. Zero, I believe, is the correct answer. He has never had his tongue in any of our fucking movies.

Index

141

Printed by BoD™in Norderstedt, Germany